Help Wanted: The First Guide to High-Tech Jobs

Help Wanted:
The First Guide
to High-Tech Jobs

Sue Hoover

ANDREWS AND MᶜMEEL, INC.
A Universal Press Syndicate Company
Kansas City   New York

Library of Congress Cataloging in Publication Data

Hoover, Sue, 1946-
Help wanted.

Includes index.
1. United States—Occupations. 2. High technology industries—United
States. 3. Job hunting—United States. I. Title.
HF5382.5.U5H66   1983   621.381'7'02373   83-15916
ISBN 0-8362-2619-4
ISBN 0-8362-2620-8 (pbk.)

Contents

CHAPTER **1**

The Jobs Revolution

"Wouldn't it be a shame after we had eliminated work
if we found out that it was really important?"

Dr. Harvey McMains
Houston Area Research Center
The Woodlands, Texas

John is not his real name. But he really exists. And so do millions like
him.

He moved up north from a small town in Missouri in 1964 to go to work
in a factory. He followed family who had come up over the years before
him. They told him there were lots of jobs and good pay, and they were
right. He started working right away in one of the factory's worst jobs—the
paint department—at $78 a week. It was a better job than he could have
gotten back home. He joined the union because it was a closed shop. After
only six months, he was laid off for the first time.

Before he was recalled, he was drafted. He served two years. When he
came home, he went to the factory and got his job back in the paint
department.

In 1969, he went to the sheet metal fabricating department and in the
next couple of years became a press operator. In the early 1970s, the
company adopted a new policy of promoting some management from rank
and file instead of hiring it all from the outside. John was selected.

There was a certain pride associated with working for an American
company that was setting the world standard for its product line. And
admittedly John was proud that he had gotten so far in the company.

In 1983, John is thirty-eight years old and making $35,000 a year as a
first line supervisor. Before a thirteen-week plant shutdown in late 1982,
he had been a lead foreman. But when the factory reopened, all but one lead
foreman in the plant were eliminated. John was demoted to keep a job.

Today, robots handle the painting job that was John's start in the
business. At one time his plant employed five thousand people. Today, it
employs fewer than two thousand. In the late 1970s—in the good days—the
plant turned out eleven thousand pieces of equipment in a year. In 1983, it
will make, maybe, four thousand.

When the plant actually closed its doors for nearly four months, people
who had worked there for thirty and thirty-five years got worried. They

The Jobs Revolution   *1*

knew it was different from the temporary layoffs of the past. Of those who were recalled, no one had less than fourteen years' seniority.

John says a lot of people seem anxious to do a job now rather than just make it through eight hours to get a paycheck. Somehow, they believe if everyone works, it helps.

Even though John sees dozens of his friends unemployed and unable to find work as good as they had at the plant, he refuses to admit that it might happen to him. If the company cuts back any more, it might as well close, he says. And he staunchly believes it won't close.

When you ask John what's going on in the American work place, he becomes angry and blames the Japanese. It's certainly true that his factory will have to compete with foreign products from this point on. But John's smart. He knows deep down everything that's gone wrong in his factory. He knows men haven't been putting in a good day's work. He knows the union will always be in the way of real change. He knows that the piece-work system, rather than offering incentives for more work, actually keeps men from working. Day after day and year after year, he has watched and participated in the charades and tricks of the trade to avoid work.

As a supervisor, he knows that the workers know that he hasn't been fooled by the silly games. But until now nobody has done anything about them. And even now, it could be too little too late.

Time will tell about John and his job at the factory. One thing is certain. Many of his friends are gone and won't return. John says sadly some are waiting, picking up a dollar where they can. There are no twenty-year-olds working in the factory, and it's unlikely there will be—unless they come sometime in the future to run the new, more complex machinery—the robots, the automation.

This book is for John, for his friends who took lower-paying jobs and for his friends who are still waiting to be recalled. It's for John's sons and daughters who must find their own way in a new job market unknown to John. And it's for all other working Americans who want to stay vital in the changing American job market.

Not only are things topsy-turvy in John's factory—but in many parts of the country, dramatic changes in the way we work, the jobs we are doing, and the products we are making have already transpired. It is not unreasonable to call it a Jobs Revolution.

As a training specialist for Sperry puts it: "It's happened already, and lots of people weren't there to catch the train."

Ned Huffman, executive director of the prestigious and successful Research Triangle Park in North Carolina, relates this anecdote:

"Now when I was a boy in Indiana—and that's been a long time ago—

many of my relatives were on farms, and many of those people went to Detroit. Why did they go to Detroit? Because Henry Ford was paying five dollars as the wage. In what? In high technology industry. So, we're not dealing with a new subject. We're dealing with an old subject.''

It's true. Most working Americans have heard or seen it somewhere—on a talk show or at a corner newsstand. "We're moving from an industrial age to a technological age.'' The transition, goes the rhetoric, is nothing new. It's akin to the move from agriculture to industry at the turn of the century.

But look at John. He's an average working American who was on the tail end of the move from agriculture to industry. And in less than twenty short years, just as he began to reap the rewards of the industrial age, he's becoming a victim of the technological age. John is naming a lot of scapegoats to avoid facing such mind-boggling change.

For one thing, like many of his unemployed coworkers, John is waiting for "things to turn around'' economically.

Indeed the economy could be blamed on first look for record unemployment levels and company failures. But with the economy on the upswing again it becomes more and more clear that what we're really dealing with in the jobs area is a full-scale revolution—a revolution far more dynamic, if only because of its speed, than the industrialization of America.

Technology, high technology, is spurring it on. It is the force that is rapidly creating new industries and recreating old industries. In the process, totally new jobs, like systems engineer, numeric control operator, and laser technician are being created while old jobs are disappearing or changing forever.

Perhaps more significant, along with the evolving technology are coming new ways of working. Many plants are outmoded not only by a lack of latest production technology, but by a propensity to avoid work. And that makes retraining a very complicated task.

Changes in the work place have been so rapid and so dramatic that high technology has become a buzz word from coast to coast. Every local political council from Texas to Michigan views it as an economic savior. Yet, no one, no one in Washington or Research Triangle Park or Lansing, Michigan, can clearly define high technology.

"High tech? I guess high tech is anything I don't understand,'' laughs Leo Zuniga, project director for the San Antonio Economic Development Council, which is attracting high-tech industries.

John Gray, at the Austin Chamber of Commerce, says: "It's probably something that takes more than minimal skills to handle.''

George Groneman at Sperry in Salt Lake City says: "It's not just the manufacturer of high-tech products. It's the end user—the banks, the schools, the grocery stores. Everything is ultimately going to be touched by high tech.''

Warren Laux, director of the Pinellas Vocational Technical Institute in Florida, agrees: "High tech is meeting the state of the art in whatever area—from high-tech industries to construction."

The state of California is trying to define high technology in an employment study and so far, has come up with the following industries as representing high tech: Computers, communication equipment, electronics components, instruments, basic high technology, and computer services. At the very least, I would add biomedicine and microelectronics.

Harry Gray, chairman of the board of United Technologies, envisions high tech permeating all existing industries that will survive the 1980s.

High tech will be used by the company that gains a competitive edge in its field—for example, a jet engine maker who uses a microelectronic chip to make his engine's gas mileage superior to others.

Meanwhile, a young engineer, just laid off from a Midwestern industrial plant, was asked what he knew about high tech:

"Not much more than that I want to get into it because everybody says it's the new thing. I'll find out."

Ned Huffman's perspective on high technology as simply progress or change may well be the best. It embodies all the evolutionary characteristics of new companies with funny-sounding names, like Paradyne or Signetics. And it also encompasses the new ways of working in old companies, like quality circles at General Motors.

Working Americans—blue collar, white collar, unskilled laborer to chief executive officer—need a clear, consistent definition of high tech if they are to face change and get on with adapting. Let me suggest the following:

> **High technology in the work place is the force that is creating new scientific data which when applied result in new industries producing new products and requiring workers with new skills and attitudes about their work. Further, it is the force that is creating new ways of producing old products and thus requires retrained and converted workers there as well.**

If you think high tech hasn't affected your job yet, think again, carefully. Because it's easy to wake up one morning on the job it seems you started only yesterday and find yourself operating in a high-tech world. Take the newspaper reporter's job, for instance.

I started writing obituaries fewer than twenty years ago working on a manual upright typewriter at a typical newspaper that set hot type on Linotype machines. Copy boys carried stories from desk to desk and to the composing room.

Today the vast majority of reporters write electronically on VDT screens and push buttons to transmit their stories to a similar screen on their editor's lesk. Type is formatted and readied for printing in the same computerized machine.

The copy boys, now called copy carriers, are all but gone. (The *Denver Post* has two of twelve left to run errands.) And the composing room jobs have changed dramatically.

What's more, entire newspapers, like the *Philadelphia Bulletin* and the *Washington Star* are gone! They've all had to compete for advertising revenue which now must be shared with the local "electronic media"—like the new high-tech television stations.

That brings us to another critical question facing the factory. Will so-called smokestack industries disappear from this country altogether? Some say yes.

And there's a lot of evidence to suggest movement in that direction. The United Auto Workers, for instance, had 759,870 members working for American automobile manufacturers in 1978. In the first quarter of 1983, more than one-third of them—269,454—were laid off indefinitely. The total number of UAW workers went from 1.5 million in the 1970s to 1.1 million in 1983.

The same percentages hold true in the steel industry, which supplies raw materials for the autos. Of 1.2 million members in 1978, the United Steel Workers reported only 775,000 working in 1983.

And all agree—the companies, the unions, and the workers themselves—that many won't ever return to work.

The question is, why won't they go back?

In the case of autos, the companies and the union have come up with a pat answer. Things were going great in the late 1970s—12 million new cars rolled off the lines in Detroit in 1978. Nobody wanted small cars. The UAW claims that two hundred thousand Hondas were sitting on the West Coast unsold. People still wanted the big car.

But then the oil crunch came with the hostage crisis in Iran. And suddenly, overnight, so the scenario goes, Americans wanted small cars, had to buy small cars in order to pay to gas them. Of course, the auto industry was caught in a squeeze. They were tooled to capacity for big cars, which were selling at big profits. And without computer aided design systems (which were available then and which they all have now), retooling was a lengthy process requiring at least a couple of years.

The American auto industry wasn't rushing change. They had been riding on top. Workers were happy with all the overtime they could handle and better pay negotiated with every union contract. Pay averages for blue-collar auto workers have been quoted as high as $27 an hour.

Enter the Japanese small car. And the rest is history.

As gas prices have stabilized and consumers once again started car shopping, another story emerged. Side by side, the American car didn't match the quality of a Japanese model. Stories of intentional sabotage on the auto assembly lines by workers and lackadaisical standards by management leaked out.

Henry Ford II said the American automobile industry got very sloppy in the 1970s, built some very, very poor quality vehicles.

General Motors said when you're on top you get lazy.

Chrysler Corporation almost went out of business.

The UAW said: "Over the years, the auto industry got lazy. The companies didn't concern themselves enough about quality; they cared only about quantity. The reason was if you were a plant manager, you were judged on getting the product out."

David Mitchell, spokesman for the union continued: "Our members told these horror stories about going to their foreman and saying, hey, there's a problem with this job. It's not right. And he'd say, leave it for the dealer; just get it out the door. And there are stories like that all over the place."

So fingers pointed back and forth about quality and whose fault it was.

But let me pose another scenario.

The auto industry put its first robots to work on the line—welding and painting—in the early 1960s. They led the way in new manufacturing technology. In the early 1970s materials other than heavy steel—various plastic composites primarily—were available and were being used sparingly for bumpers and doors and other car parts to lighten weight and cut gas mileage.

So, why did the auto industry allow itself to get caught so off guard in November of 1979 when an unstable country like Iran did what it had held the cards to do for years?

I believe there was a stalemate on high-tech retooling—a stalemate between union and company. The company never made technology a priority issue. Everytime it broached the subject, the union said what about our jobs? While everybody made money, nobody pushed the issue. When the gas crisis hit, and the American consumer suddenly looked around at an international auto marketplace and found a better deal, the companies decided they had to revolutionize their technologies overnight. And the UAW had no choice but to buy it.

Now, let's also look at that competitive international marketplace. For autos, and other products as well, our competition has been Japan. If we ask John why the Japanese build better products, he says, "Well, they probably have their employees very involved. Maybe they even are stockholders in the company. . . . But they don't have our same circumstances. We blew their country up thirty years ago. So everything they have has got to be fairly new, geared to high productivity. When that goes up, cost goes down."

John is basically correct. A lot of what Japan as well as many other emerging industrial nations have today, are things Americans gave them after the war—including a man named Deming.

W. Edwards Deming, an American, is a household word today in corporate headquarters from John Deere to General Motors. In 1950, he took a concept of quality control to the Japanese. At that time, if you recall, "Made in Japan" was synonomous with shoddy. It took years to smooth out the working systems, but today quality in the Japanese workplace is a way of life.

Deming, now in his eighties and the namesake for an annual quality award in Japan, says Americans still haven't learned the essence of quality control. Part of what goes into that essence is what I call a new work discipline, the subject of a later chapter of this book. It comes, in part, from being hungry, struggling to compete—something American smokestack industries, always on top, haven't had to do until now.

But I don't think smokestack industries are going to disappear in America.

They are going to start competing in the global marketplace that's been building, with our help, for years. And to compete, they must adopt high technology. Right now, high tech in smokestack industries means cost-efficient machines doing the work high-cost human labor used to do. . . . Not just the physical work on the line, but the paper-pushing that grew to exorbitant proportions in middle management.

Randy Woods, an executive of the Woodlands, a model community in Houston, and a former executive at Bethlehem Steel, is in a minority in America, having had experience in both old-style industries and new-style high-tech industries:

"I think they [smokestack industries] will survive, but I believe that they will emerge from this downturn in a very different mode. I think that they will be leaner obviously. And I think they will specialize in those product lines that will make money for them. . . . They just can't be all things to all people anymore. We will still need a basic production sector in this country, but it will be more automation, less labor."

There will be new jobs created—like robotics technician to repair and maintain and program the robots. But unfortunately the labor force which is being discarded isn't ready to step into the new job slots.

The most dramatic part of the fall of smokestack industries is the simultaneous meteoric rise of high-tech industries, called sunrise industries. Smokestacks are diminishing in the Midwest and Northeast, while literally hundreds of high-tech companies are flourishing in the Sun Belt and West. But there's very little crosstalk.

My dad was born in 1901 in the tiny farming town of Brighton, Iowa. In his seventy-eight years, he never bought the Industrial Revolution. When he was a boy, the family moved to town. Farming had become less lucrative than my grandfather's job building the railroad which was the technology of the day connecting East to West.

For a number of years while I was growing up, Dad worked in a small factory we called the "shop." But he never joined a union or adopted the values of industrialized work life.

He didn't take to many newfangled ideas. He flew in an airplane only once in his life, and he never really adjusted to automobiles. Twentieth-century pace was just too much for him. In almost eighty years, my dad couldn't pull himself out of the simple life he loved and remembered in Brighton.

But now consider John. He left a farming community just as my dad, went to work in the city in a factory, adapted just fine, and in only twenty years, he's out of step again. The world is speeding by him.

John is like many American workers today—both blue-collar physical laborer and white-collar middle manager—who aren't ready to make a quantum leap to high tech. Furthermore, high tech may not ever need or want all of them.

Consider the situation. The typical UAW worker and steel worker and most other smokestack-industry workers including management are working second generation in basically the same plant. They've worked under a union-run environment built on a combative relationship between company and worker, a condition which does little for the work ethic. In the meantime, as a nation, we've ignored the workers' education. They don't have the basics, math and science, which they need for the new job world of high technology. They didn't need them in the past. We had granted them more and more dollars to stay in the system and supply the backbreaking or paper-pushing labor that was needed at the moment.

Our value system of work in this country has become so fouled up that a four-year college graduate may disregard his or her studied profession and become a bus driver because a union contract assures higher wages. There are two problems. One is that many young college students are in courses of study that do nothing to prepare them for today's work place. The other is that wages in a host of jobs in this country have grown disproportionately to the actual value of the task.

Furthermore, now we are deciding we simply don't need as many old-style physical laborers and middle managers. And that raises some very basic questions. For instance, who decides who works and who doesn't? And is work a privilege or a burden? And of those who don't work, how will they function economically?

Technology, as inevitable as it is, makes us, as a free-thinking society, consider certain ramifications.

Dr. Harvey McMains was on the team of scientists at Bell Laboratories in the late 1940s that developed the transistor. It revolutionized the development of electronics—putting the industry on a fast track that has yet to put on the brakes.

In the spring of 1983, Dr. McMains was named to head the Houston Area Research Center (HARC), the research group housed in Research Forest at the Woodlands.

He has given a lot of thought to the fundamental nature of work and its value to man:

"Deep in my heart, I don't think people enjoy being on welfare. I think they want to work."

So we must ask ourselves: "Should we advance technology to the point that we take people out of the equation?"

And if so, "Wouldn't it be a shame after we had eliminated work if we found out it was really important?"

Dr. McMains says we should be using new technologies to create work—not get rid of it.

He sees trade—an expansion of the global marketplace—as one way to better utilize research and create new industries and jobs.

"Our research in this country has been very successful at winning Nobel Prizes, but we're not discovering things that would satisfy real needs in the world," says Dr. McMains.

For example, "For political reasons we've taken the most productive land out of production when we could be furthering research to keep food longer so we can produce it and develop trade with other nations who are hungry."

Likewise, Dr. McMains thinks we should concentrate on developing industries which suit those undeveloped countries and put their people to work. The solution to the Mexican "undocumented worker" in this country, he says, is to help Mexico develop work for its people.

As grandiose and possibly politically unpopular as Dr. McMains' theories are, he says he is devoting the rest of his intellectual life to supporting and developing them at HARC.

"What I wish I had been more aware of is that science and technology are only valuable when they serve society. The idea of seeking knowledge for knowledge's sake was only possible in my day because the economy was good. . . . We no longer are so rich that we don't have to worry about the society that technology serves. We have to worry about people who don't have jobs."

Think for a moment about the second or third question you ask of someone sitting near you on an airplane. "What do you do?"

The answer to that question defines who we are. Our work is an integral part of our makeup. It offers a purpose and challenge to our lives.

Women are finally coming out of the house to fulfill new dimensions of their lives with work. Ask any unemployed person what it's like without work, and most will tell you they're lost, they have no self-esteem.

So, yes, we must worry about people who don't have jobs. But we must worry for more than esoteric reasons.

Our smokestack industries by and large have provided a stable economic base in this country since World War II. By their success, this country has been able to lead the world, set the standards, pursue intellectual breakthroughs. Those pursuits are still flourishing and in fact developing into a very substantial new-style industry which we call high tech.

Computers, microelectronics, and spaceships are all products of full-fledged industries now. They have different ways of doing things which are changing the way we work in all industries.

They have by and large set their own fast track and, once on it, few look back. They need people to work in their industries, a new breed of worker who's technical, committed, and usually young. So far, they've found workers while carefully steering clear of those who could be misfits in their newly created workplaces.

But now the time is coming when they must deal with the misfits. The successful high-tech industries may be the only ones who can address the problem because they're the only ones who understand fully who and what are needed in the new work place. Most old-style industries truly don't grasp the changes, and they're too poor to affect them anyway. Don't look to Washington. The federal government is a classic old-style set-up. So high tech, no matter how smooth its fast track forward, must look back and help to solve problems it has created inadvertently.

Dr. McMains said research flourished because the economy was good. That luxury is past. Not only have millions of American jobs disappeared already in the Jobs Revolution—with millions more like John's on the line—but millions of middle-class incomes which purchased middle-class goods and services have gone as well. And until we find work for the millions of displaced workers in this country who have been supporting the economy—albeit with unjustifiably high wages—the economy will not allow technology to continue to evolve at its current speed.

I had this conversation with a Washington, D.C., adviser to Congress on high technology . . .

Q: Will manufacturing move offshore?

A: Yes, a good bit of it. There's no reason why it shouldn't. Lord knows the Third World needs jobs.

Q: I defy you to tell that to a GM or John Deere worker.

A: There's nothing sacred about an assembly line job.

Q: Well, there is something becoming sacred about a *job,* and those people who are losing their jobs are threatened by those Third World countries. It's a hot potato.

A: True. But we can't deal with the millions of workers unemployed at the expense of the firms that create the jobs.

CHAPTER **2**

The New Geography of Jobs

"Governor, let me ask you a question.
Who in the hell would want to move to Michigan?"

Ned Huffman	to:
Research Triangle Park	former Michigan
North Carolina	Governor William Milliken

Not more than a generation ago, people were moving off farms, many of them in the South, and heading for factory jobs on new "high-tech" assembly lines in the Northeast and Midwest. Now that generation's children are heading to the Sun Belt, the new land of plenty where today's high-tech business is settling.

They don't all understand the new business, and it's harder to get jobs in it than it was in the auto plants. But more and more people every day are finding ways to settle there. They may end up taking lower paying wages to get in the door. Or they may find jobs in the growing service industries supporting the employees and families of the new core industries.

The 1980 census shows that, for the first time in the history of the United States, more people (117.6 million) live in the South and West than in the old industrialized Northeast and North Central regions (108 million). From 1975 to 1980, some 3.2 million people left the Northeast and North Central states. In the same period, the same number moved into the South and West. That's a rate of 1,750 people a day. It continued through 1981 at the same rate.

The migration is established. And more and more people will follow—some informed, others not.

The Great States Battle for Jobs is on. But there's really no contest.

Far in the lead of the fifty-state race are places nicknamed Silicon Mountain, Silicon Prairie, Silicon Hills, Silicon Desert, not to mention Silicon Gulch and Ceramic Valley.

The front-runners are almost all in the nation's Sun Belt and West. The prize: the new, clean, affluent high-tech industries looking for locations to set up satellite operations. The states all agree that if you're looking for jobs today, you're looking for high tech. Many high-tech companies are headquartered in Silicon Valley, California—named for its concentration of high-tech industries making and using silicon chips. Part of the states' campaigns to pull in the business, and thus the jobs, is to acquire the silicon image tied, of course, to the quality of life particular to that location.

And so, Colorado Springs, Colorado, is Silicon Mountain; North Dallas, Texas, is Silicon Prairie; Austin, Texas, prefers Silicon Hills; Phoenix and Tucson, Arizona, are Silicon Desert.

Ceramic Valley was adopted by San Diego, California, in an ad campaign. Ceramic is the newest state-of-the-art material used for packaging electronic chips, among other product applications. Some of the major manufacturers are in San Diego.

Quality of life is a major factor in the battle for jobs and high-tech industry. The companies are looking for places where they can attract the engineers who are instrumental commodities to high tech just as mass labor was to industrial companies in years past. The engineers are picky, according to company recruiters. They want a work place that offers peace of mind for fostering think tanks. That comes only with pleasant surroundings like lakes, hills, temperate climates. They also want recreational opportunities close by. Skiing is probably the number one demand. Some who are selling Texas go so far as to include Colorado skiing as one of their advantages—since it's so close by airline.

In addition to ski areas, the quality of life checklist includes golf courses. Salt Lake City claims to have twice the average number of golf and tennis courts per capita. On the other hand, emphasizing quality not quantity, Houston's Woodlands imported white sand from Florida to fill the traps in its golf course.

One of Colorado Springs' major high-tech industrial areas is located on Garden of the Gods Road, less than a quarter-mile from the entrance to Garden of the Gods Park, a longtime tourist attraction. It's nestled against a dramatic backdrop of the Rockies just a few miles from towering Pike's Peak.

Quality of life was one of the biggest reasons the high-tech business started in California, still the undeniable home of this country's electronics industry. But things have changed in Silicon Valley. For one thing it's grown. It now stretches from San Jose in the south to Palo Alto in the north. The narrow valley, once a sparsely populated series of prune orchards, has become overcrowded, housing costs have outreached even some of the most highly paid engineers, driving is a drag, and the smog is worse.

So, as high-tech companies have expanded, they've looked to the hinterlands in order to attract the engineers and to cut their own costs for expansion. For a variety of reasons, the hinterland has turned out to be Sun Belt and West. The jobs statistics tell the story.

• Sperry in Salt Lake City just became the area's largest employer with 4,100 employees, overtaking the depressed mines.

• Austin, Texas, has added thirty thousand manufacturing jobs since it started targeting high tech seventeen years ago. Another estimated ninety thousand jobs have followed in support and service areas.

• Hewlett-Packard announced plans in 1982 to build a manufacturing complex north of Denver along Colorado's Front Range that could ultimately employ sixteen thousand people.

The list is endless. The point is jobs are there, and the population is shifting from the old industrialized Northeast and Midwest to the Sun Belt to take advantage of them.

Sun Belt cities are welcoming the growth—and the by-product jobs in grocery stores, movie theaters, home building, etc. From Tucson to Salt Lake City, brand new look-alike industrial parks with street names like Research Drive and Computer Lane are springing up near walled housing developments built to attract the engineers.

Economic development councils from dozens of front-runner communities are raiding and prospecting for new industry and the jobs that go with them. Each claims an active file of some one hundred different companies.

Salt Lake City claims it formed the first "raiding party" to venture to Silicon Valley in search of new business in the 1960s. But Brad Bertoch at the Chamber says the game quickly got too heavy for Utah. The state simply couldn't match the prospecting budgets anted up by some wealthier states.

"Besides," says Bertoch, "if you go to Silicon Valley and throw a cocktail party now, nobody will come because forty-nine other states are doing the same thing."

Most of the Sun Belt competitors agree. The trick now, they say, is to get corporate expansion people to come to them for a visit.

"If we can get 'em here, we can sell 'em," was the confident conclusion in San Diego, Tucson, Phoenix, San Antonio, Austin, Colorado Springs, Salt Lake City, Albuquerque, and Tampa.

As significant as quality of life is, there are, of course, other factors that affect the selection of new locations for high-tech companies. The following were confirmed as critical company concerns by representatives of the cities and states with the most success at recruiting.

• TRANSPORTATION—Whether it's a new high-tech business or an old-style smokestack business, they've got to be able to move raw materials into the manufacturing area and the products back out to market. In the case of high tech, however, usually the goods are very small and pose much less of a transportation problem. It's much easier, for instance, to move thousands of silicon chips than thousands of automobiles. So, the high-tech business is not limited to locating by a waterway or major railway. Companies do make sure, however, that the intended facility site can offer good interstate travel by truck and good rail service.

The transportation issue that most concerns high-tech companies is air transportation for people in and out of the satellite facility. The company sometimes sets its requirements in terms of time traveling from headquarters in Silicon Valley to the new location. That time might be two hours, and it's all right with the company if the travel is by airline, corporate jet, or car—just so it's two hours.

One of the problems some of the new Sun Belt high-tech communities have is that commercial airlines don't serve them well. Bill Davis at the Committee of 100 in Pinellas County, Florida, says most California companies have an aversion to coming east of the Mississippi anyway. And then, if they can't get a nonstop flight to their destination, it can sour a deal.

Davis says Florida often gets "short-stopped" when an airline carrying a company site selector from California stops in Houston or Dallas or Austin. Many times, he says, the company representative looks around on his layover and stays.

• ACADEMIC ENVIRONMENT—Research is the key element in the start-up of many high-tech companies. It fosters the ideas that foster the new product concepts. So, entrepreneurs settle around universities and ultimately open their doors as companies, creating jobs in the process.

In addition, many companies choose to locate around a good university which can supply the professionals, usually engineers, necessary to their business.

Both factors are responsible for at least two major high-technology growth areas in the country—Silicon Valley around Stanford University in Palo Alto, California, and Route 128, which circles Boston near Massachusetts Institute of Technology (MIT). The Boston area is one of the few thriving high-tech areas not in the Sun Belt. It shows the strength of an exceptional academic environment.

The other classic example of high tech and academics working together is North Carolina's Research Triangle Park. The development, begun in the 1950s, is a leader in the high-tech race today. The 5,500-acre park is built in the center of the "Golden Triangle"—with Duke University in Durham, University of North Carolina in Chapel Hill, and North Carolina State in Raleigh at each point.

But companies don't just want the high-end academics for engineering talent. They also look for vocational education support in communities where they plan to open facilities. Since most high-tech companies require so many skilled employees below the engineering level, they want a local school where they can get a ready supply. The most successful situation is when the company works hand in hand with a school—often supplying visiting teachers and expensive equipment—to offer potential future employees customized training for that company.

• RIGHT-TO-WORK ENVIRONMENT—Quite bluntly, the high-tech companies don't want unions. They don't even want to go to a community which has had a lot of organizing activity. They feel a harmful, combative, irreversible relationship has evolved between unions and companies that is not in keeping with the high-tech industry's no-nonsense fast track.

That's another major reason high tech is settling in the Sun Belt, where unions have been generally unsuccessful, and most states have right-to-work laws. Many high-tech companies won't even consider locating in the unionized Northeast and Midwest no matter what the other attractions.

• INEXPENSIVE, DEDICATED LABOR—The Sun Belt communities are certainly not working as hard as they are to attract high-tech industry just to get jobs for the Northerners who are going there. They're doing it, almost without exception, to offer jobs to their own residents who in the past have typically had to leave home to go up north to find jobs.

The companies welcome the homegrown Sun Belt labor force that not only wants to work, but has been unspoiled by the excesses lavished on Northern labor over the years. The companies are looking for a new work discipline on the part of all workers—from engineer to assembler. This is, I believe, the most cataclysmic change in our workplace and job market.

It's also a matter of economics. The high-tech companies, which, since their inception, have had to compete with foreign goods, say they must keep labor costs down. And the Sun Belt historically has had cheaper labor.

• POLITICAL ENVIRONMENT—More and more high-tech companies want to meet with local and state political leaders, say the community economic development promoters. They're looking for a stable political climate. They want to know first that the climate is favorable to business, and then that the climate won't change any time soon.

By and large, they're looking for low taxes, cooperative zoning, and educational facilities to support a skilled labor force.

• LAND—Most new-style companies, for aesthetic and cost reasons, select a suburban location where they can buy a minimum of forty or fifty acres. Obviously, that land isn't even available in places like Silicon Valley anymore, not to mention how much it might cost. But it's no problem in places like Colorado Springs, where Chamber officials say they could spread eastward to Kansas if necessary.

Some communities are giving land away as part of the enticement to select their location.

• QUALITY OF LIFE—The companies want everything from a "safe," suburban lifestyle to cultural and recreational facilities to reasonably priced housing to good weather. (Good weather, by the way, means warmth and sunshine.) When it comes down to the nitty gritty, companies say the quality of life is the crucial issue that tells whether they get the high-tech talent. And most say that talent makes all the difference in whether the company succeeds.

Research Triangle Park in North Carolina has been among the most successful in attracting high-tech industry. Ned Huffman, the executive director in charge of new business that goes into the park, says hundreds of executives from other states, including several governors, have come to the park looking for its secret to success.

He doesn't believe some are in the high-tech ballgame.

"Governor Milliken [former governor of Michigan] was here," related Huffman. "And we had a very friendly conversation. But finally, I said, 'Governor, who in the hell would move to Michigan?' He said, 'That's a very fair question; that's what I'm here for. I'm trying to find something that will give us a new thrust.'"

Michigan's high-tech solution has been the formation of three independent research institutes operating in conjunction with three of its major universities. Millions of dollars have been earmarked for setting up the institutes and an accompanying program to encourage entrepreneural activity in the state.

But if you review the companies' checklist for location requirements, you'll find Michigan doesn't meet a lot of the criteria—especially regarding the quality of life and union issues.

"Companies are spending their money somewhere, and they want to be sure they're getting the best return on it," said Huffman. "Are they going to go to Michigan where only fifty of one hundred questions [about the location site] have positive answers? What about the climate there? What about the political climate? What about taxation? What about unions there? And you can go on."

But those questions haven't stopped a lot of other unlikely states either. The Office of Technology Assessment, a research agency for Congress, is working on a report about the activity going on in various states to attract high tech.

In preliminary information, it reports thirty-eight different state-sponsored programs have been launched in twenty-two states in the last three years. Among the states seeking high tech are Iowa, Illinois, Indiana, Ohio, Nebraska, and Kansas.

Leo Zuniga in San Antonio, a community relatively successful in attracting high tech despite a lack of a good university system and lots of money, thinks states like Michigan may have a shot. He calls Michigan's dollar commitment, respected academics, and venture capital financing available for start-up companies a phenomenal package.

Jim Haynes, president of the Phoenix Chamber of Commerce, also sees a limit to the Sun Belt's unchallenged heyday:

"The governments in the Northeast which have in the past been very happy, have sat there and looked at a bunch of smokestacks and said, 'Where are they gonna move?' The problem is the world's passed that guy by already. That's not who you're worried about anymore. That guy is just playing out his hand till it comes up all deuces. But increasingly those states are becoming our competition. They're seeing it. They have to diversify."

But others well into high-tech development, like John Scott, Wake County (Raleigh, North Carolina) planner, say Northern states trying to get on the high-tech bandwagon are scrambling with too little, too late:

"The Northeast has been slow to realize what's happening and then to respond. There's almost an attitude of, "Why would people leave us for a place like North Carolina?"

Indeed, many people who live in big urban centers in the Northeast today are real geographic snobs. They complain day in and day out about the livability of places like Detroit, Cleveland, New York, Chicago. But they can't imagine any sophisticated person leaving.

When I left Detroit some seven years ago to move to Colorado, I remember friends insisting I was abandoning the ship, giving up the cause—the urban cause to turn around the city. It was all happening in the city, they said. What could I possibly find in Colorado?

When I first moved to Detroit, I remember justifying the fact that I lived in miserable weather with dreadful pollution and a combat zone kind of criminal environment because of the people—my friends, my peers, some of the finest journalists in the country. But today it's hard to ignore that many of them are editors in California, Arizona, and Florida.

Meanwhile the Northeast will be hard pressed to maintain the infrastructure—the roads, schools, municipal services—it has now, according to Scott's vision of the future. It will have to adjust to no growth after years of industrial-based growth. Some towns up north are already and others will become "municipal vegetables," said Scott.

They may become attractive for fourth- or fifth-generation manufacturing, like making the cabinets to house computers or the staples to hold the shipping crates together. "That's the labor market up there," he said.

But it's unlikely that new industries will pay union labor $15 an hour for those products. So, that manufacturing, too, might be moved offshore for economics' sake.

My first indication that this wasn't business as usual was during an interview in Research Triangle Park in North Carolina. The phone started ringing.

On each call after several minutes of patient listening to the other end, the "boss" said, "Well, it's not going to get any better, so go on home, do what you think you have to do."

At my next interview, an escort met me in the lobby. We walked down a long corridor—on my right, a wall of glass with a view into a meticulously groomed courtyard and on my left, offices. Dozens of people had come out of their offices and were pressed against the glass. Finally, one of the people looked nervously at my escort: "Well, what's the word?"

"There'll be an announcement at one o'clock," she replied.

Then she turned to me, shaking her head, "We'll never close. There are too many Yankees here now."

It was snowing.

And in the past, in North Carolina, when it snowed, everything closed. The snow that day wasn't even sticking. Granted it was snowing hard, but it was melting on sidewalks and roads. Nonetheless, native Carolinians don't like snow.

I later found out that several events planned for that March day had been cancelled the crystal clear night before when the weatherman issued the snow forecast. Within an hour of the first snowflake, all the schools were closed and kids piled onto buses to get them home safe and sound.

The business I visited closed on time that afternoon, but my escort had been very accurate when she made the remark about Yankees. She herself was from Kingston, New York. Her boss, too, was from upstate New York although he had been in North Carolina for almost twenty years. He confirmed that the company used to close on snow days, but he pointed out that it cost the company thousands of dollars in lost production time. Now, with more snow-experienced Northerners, closing was a less pressing issue.

Predictably, Northerners who are moving south for jobs are finding they must make adjustments to a new lifestyle. But their adjustments are certainly no more than the Southerners are making to accommodate all those Yankees in town.

One of the biggest accommodations that faces the majority of Sun Belt and Western boom towns is water. The reason the Sun Belt can accept high-tech industries is that the industries themselves require little water— with the exception of semiconductor manufacturers, many of whom now recycle the water they use. However, with the increased populations that come to work in high-tech industries—the most affluent of whom want lush green lawns in desert communities—water becomes an issue for the "locals" to contemplate. Water has been responsible for some communities adopting a no-growth attitude.

In Tucson, where they say they have the lowest per capita use of water in the nation, economic developer Bill Stephenson says the way to control water usage is to put a price tag on it. Needless to say, there's a conservationist attitude in place in Tucson.

Likewise in Denver, the water board has issued alternate watering days for years—even when snowfall in the mountains has been good. After all, Denver is actually a desert too.

Jim Haynes in Phoenix has the same attitude about his city: "We live in a desert. We've got to be conscious about water. If we're not, we are not being honest with the future of our region."

At some point, says Haynes, communities like Phoenix will have to come up with a formula for the number of gallons of water it will give to run an industry in exchange for the number of jobs. The Chamber recently discouraged a food processor that would have used 1.7 million gallons of water a day in exchange for 250 jobs. Not a good trade-off, said Haynes.

Most growing Sun Belt communities are building water projects to service the daily needs of the populations. And they believe, with careful monitoring, the water shortages can be controlled.

So, the new boom towns are accommodating the newcomers. And generally, the Northerners seem to be adapting well to the slower Southern pace, despite remnants of geographic snobbishness. One hotel manager, transferred to open a new Sun Belt chain hotel, said he found the local people there unfriendly and not very bright. After a while though, he said, they became much more friendly.

A radio talk show host in Denver, originally from Brooklyn, New York, renamed Denver "Ken and Barbie Doll Town" because he said the young people who predominantly live there have no sense of urban responsibility.

A black company manager who transferred to Arizona from the Midwest, however, said he thought the conservative images he had about the people in the West proved to be more fiscal than social.

There was one major reported clash of locals and newcomers in Phoenix though. Haynes at the Chamber claimed the problems in the much-reported Tent City there were because the new poor coming from up north with no jobs or means of support were not getting along with the traditional winos who winter in Phoenix and feel the streets are their established territory.

CHAPTER 3

The New Work Place

"In all candor, I think the thing that has forced the change is that
employers who weren't unionized saw what happened to those who got
unionized, and they said, we don't want that, so we need to change."

Jesse Flores
Datapoint Corporation
San Antonio, Texas

Every morning at 7:00 sharp they line up in rows in the parking lot—the only place large enough for the entire day shift of nine hundred to stand together. From a distance, all you see is a sea of waist-length smocks—some blue, some brown, some yellow. Closer in, you see Kyocera scripted over every left breast.

Kasey Hasegawa, president of Kyocera, steps to the front and tells them—everyone from engineer-managers to operators—how the company is faring in international competition. Some days the message is positive; some days President Hasegawa cautions them they must work harder. Every day he tells them how much their dedicated service is appreciated.

The speech is brief, maybe five minutes long, and President Hasegawa is up front only one day a week. Often, someone from the ranks, who may never have spoken to a group, is asked to tell co-workers about himself. About once a week, a safety manager offers plant safety tips.

Among other benefits, the company hopes that the sharing of information with all workers will result in an operator taking pride in telling her family she helped to build a part that runs the home washing machine.

After the address, the Kyocera plant exercises en masse—nothing strenuous, just a few toe touches and arm circles to get the blood flowing. Then it's inside to another brief meeting in smaller groups to plan the workday. President Hasegawa takes his place at the center desk in a long open office with twenty or more other desks. It's not unusual to find him still at his desk at midnight. Japanese music plays soothingly in the background.

Recognize the scene from one of those TV documentaries about the workaday world of Japan?

Well, hold onto your reading glasses. This scene is in San Diego, U.S.A. And three-quarters of the Kyocera managers are American.

The Kyocera style—company spokesmen insist it's a hybrid, not particularly Japanese or American—is unquestionably an extreme case, but it does exemplify many aspects of America's changing work place, from communication and teamwork to open offices and a time-clock honor system.

While few American managers are embracing the pure Kyocera style, it is at least arousing their curiosity because the style is spelling success. And for years in America, a company's bottom line has been the overriding indicator of how good its management is.

The world of high tech is a fast-paced, no-nonsense, globally competitive business. There's no room for counterproductive distractions. The credo is that labor does the job right, and the company treats employees as valuable resources. Thus, new-style high-tech companies are speerheading changes in the traditional work place. Old-style industries, meanwhile, are trying to implement some of the changes in an effort to mend their ailing businesses.

As one smokestack executive in Detroit said: "The economic times we've been going through have created a sense that we've got to do something even if it's wrong."

The most dramatic change is in the basic relationship between employer and employee. In new-style companies, management and labor talk to one another.

Of course, John, our first line supervisor, "talks" to the guys on the line. "Sure, I like those guys. But I don't go have a beer with them. I really don't know them that well. I don't socialize with them. There's a definite line, and I'm on this side and they're on that side. I don't enter their realm, and they don't enter mine."

There's an unwritten understanding. John stopped being one of the guys the day he stopped paying union dues.

But the new communication in the work place goes much deeper than everybody feeling like part of the gang socially. The key change is the recognition by supervisors that people working on the line have something to say legitimately in the interest of the company. For workers to want to communicate with management, they must believe that what they say is valued and respected. It's hard to come to that understanding when neither side crosses into the other's "realm."

There must be a trust, an honesty between company and employee. Over the years, that trust and communication have been eroded in old-style American business. Some say the unions turned their members against companies. Others say companies have never had a healthy respect for workers. Whatever, old-style companies and employees won't start talking to one another overnight—in spite of the number of "programs" management puts into place by traditional dictate.

At Kyocera, people spend so much time talking to one another in decision-making processes, it often seems cumbersome. Nevertheless, Bill Everitt, a vice president, says the exchange of ideas works because by the time a decision is made, everyone has bought into it.

Everitt, a traditional American executive for eighteen years, thinks at Kyocera there's a fundamental philosophical difference from the way most Americans approach work.

"At Kyocera, decisions are made only for the good of the people at the company, never for the personal career advancement of an individual. Many Americans can't cope with that philosophy. They can't be real team members.

"Most American-style managers have been groomed all their lives to be totally independent, to make decisions, to be in command, chart their own destinies. At Kyocera, we're just average people who work like the dickens," he said.

Communication is considered so vital to the new work place that the physical set-up of new-style companies has changed to reflect it.

Open offices, like the ones at Kyocera, are the extreme. Most American companies have modified the totally open office to cubicled offices. Theoretically, the cubicles offer some privacy for the sake of concentration, but still afford the informality of getting up and walking to see a co-worker without an appointment.

At some companies, like Hewlett-Packard, even the powerful division managers sit in cubicled offices—though they're twice the size of surrounding cubicles. Hewlett-Packard also coined the phrase—Management By Wandering Around (MBWA). It goes a step beyond managers having an open door policy toward employees. It encourages managers to actually walk around—going to employees instead of having them come to management.

Dispensing with the formality of private offices, with all their trappings, is intended to provide an environment in which you can talk to your supervisor and get the job done without getting bogged down in office memos and protocol.

The informality of engineers—their shirt sleeves rolled up, coffee cups in hand, chit-chatting in a cubicle over an instrument, a document, or a schematic—can lead the old-style industrial worker to wonder who's working. But the fact is they are working, in earnest, and solving problems of work without structural fanfare.

Compare that to the stuffiness of many old-style smokestack corporate headquarters where, in the past, executives have had to put on their suit coats when they left their private offices to walk down the hall to the men's room.

In the old-style environment, projects could be stalled for literally weeks awaiting an appointment with a supervisor. Highly structured meetings rarely turned out to be honest exchanges. Most middle managers restrained from offering sincere and knowledgeable input because they feared their boss would interpret it as an ill-timed power play.

The same conditions have existed at the blue-collar level. There has been little respect for what the guy on the line had to say, no open lines of communication or reason for him to try to talk. Nonetheless, he's undoubtedly had plenty to say.

Ned Huffman at Research Triangle Park used to be a district manager for Southern Bell. Although the territory extended over several states, he claims that he had a personal contact with each one of the employees working under him at least every couple of months. He said they called him Ned, and he called them by their first names.

Years later, that seemingly insignificant practice gained significance after he toured a steel plant with its chief executive officer. The CEO didn't speak to a single employee, he said. And, true to the conditioning, not a single employee even looked up to meet the CEO's eyes as they passed.

The team approach to work, based on communication, is the cornerstone of many new-style corporate philosophies. At Hewlett-Packard, headquartered in Silicon Valley, they call it the "HP Way." Many similar corporate philosophies include new practices that seemingly leave the new work place with very little structure.

For instance, employees (even hourly wage earners) in all HP plants work with "flex hours"—meaning they can come in anytime they choose between 6:00 and 8:30 in the morning. They leave eight and a half hours later. They take breaks and lunch when they need them. There are no time clocks. The only bell that rings is a gentle chime that suggests a cup of coffee on the company. The idea, says HP, is to encourage workers to get up and talk to co-workers around the coffee cart—promote communication. There's also no "quitting time" at HP since workers come and go on an honor system.

Compare that to the regimentation of the 3:00 whistle that blows at old-style factories. It signals a literal stampede of workers, lunch pails tucked under their arms, storming through plant gates and making a dash to their cars.

Some new-style high-tech companies prefer to keep some structure in their work places as a practical matter. Intel, a semiconductor manufacturer also headquartered in Silicon Valley, rejects the flex-hour concept, for instance. Company spokesmen say it leaves too narrow a window in the day when everyone is at work. It actually works against good communication because the person you want to see is seemingly never there when you are.

Mostek, part of United Technologies in Dallas, claims some people simply work better under a structured environment. Management compares today's preferred traditional, structured classroom over the experimental open classroom of the 1970s.

Despite some differences, nearly all new-style companies adhere to the credo: Respect for workers offered in exchange for a job well done. It manifests itself in honest communication and varying degrees of informality in the work place.

Finally, some companies have carried their new employer-employee communication philosophy to the parking lots. They insist that if special parking spaces are reserved for the brass, it's a carry-over of the holier-than-thou attitude, and it hampers real communication. So, no assigned parking spaces.

Even Kyocera managers drew the line on that purist attitude. Their top executives need to be able to get in and out conveniently without wasting time looking for a parking space—so they get the spots nearest the door, just as Lee Iacocca does, I'm sure.

A cable television station at the Woodlands in Houston has the great compromise on the parking lot issue. Next to the bigwigs' assigned spots was one marked "Employee of the Month."

When I visited Hewlett-Packard, company spokemen told me that not only does the honor system work with flex hours, but hourly workers, with just a few components to solder in order to finish a circuit board, would stay a few minutes beyond their eight-hour workday to finish it. It gave them a fresh start the next morning!

It seemed like company propaganda to me—simply too far removed from our well-established system of union grievances for the slightest aberration in the workday.

But as I traveled and saw the new work place in action at one high-tech company after another, I came to believe Hewlett-Packard and all the others. I posed the scenario to Jerry Turner, an assistant vice president who deals in human resources for Excello-McCord in Detroit.

He insisted that a company cannot view the new communication as just another "program"—something you can snap into place and have it take off. But, given the proper time, nurturing, and honest commitment, it can truly change the work place.

Traditionally, supervisors, or management, have planned and organized the work that is done in a company. The workers have been the doers.

Now, companies are trying to get the planning and organizational duties down into the ranks as far as possible. They call it employee involvement, or participatory management, and it only works when company and workers talk to one another. The communication groups formed are often called quality circles because a lot of what they talk about involves working better and making better products.

Kyocera feels that quality and communication are so much a part of their everyday work life they don't need quality circles.

Old-style smokestack industries, like the auto companies, are using quality circles as a starting point for launching a new-style work place.

General Motors has Employee Participation Groups in place at three-quarters of its 140 plants. Bill Kornegay, director of the elaborately organized system, says he can point to many examples of success in better work and better products as a result of the groups.

For instance, a troublesome wind noise in the window of a Buick was cured a couple of years ago when a blue-collar worker took the car for a spin on his own time and spotted the problem in the door assembly.

Ford Motor Company has some ten thousand workers in its quality circles called Employee Involvement Groups and reports similar successes.

Technology is a big reason old-style companies want to break down barriers and really talk with employees. Says Jerry Turner at Excello-McCord in Detroit:

"I think the new work environment fits very closely with the introduction of new technology. People are very clever. If you introduce a new process and if people don't view the process as something that they think makes sense, they are going to create ways to make it not work."

So, the old-style industries that are going to survive—that are going to bring high technology into their plants in order to compete globally—are going to have to talk in earnest with their employees. They must adopt policies and practices of the new work place.

Excello-McCord introduced quality circles to its gasket plant in Wyandotte, Michigan, a couple of years ago. Wyandotte is in the heart of Detroit's "downriver suburbs," where the sky is always gray. The air is often so polluted you can literally see particles in it. Wyandotte is a typical smokestack town.

The gasket plant quality circles are voluntary—about half of the three hundred employees have joined so far. In the beginning, the workers talked about housekeeping problems, things that they had wanted to grump about to somebody for years. Most of the groups have that out of their systems. Now, they're talking about things that can make a difference in how the work is performed.

They started meeting for a couple of hours a week during company time. Now they want to get more involved.

Jerry Turner is pleased. "We have a fair amount of evidence that if you give people the opportunity to do some controlling and organizing of their work, rather than just being limited to doing, they will work overtime—just as the assemblers at Hewlett-Packard. We have had people at Wyandotte come in and say they're really into this project, and they'd like to make some headway. They'd like to work some overtime. They say we don't have to pay them for it. They don't want to be paid for it. They want to come in early before the shift starts or they want to work late or come in on Saturday.

"What we hope to see is that as problems come up they will be dealt with, and better ways of doing work will be identified and put into place. We would hope to improve our cost picture but we aren't promoting it on that theme. There are a lot of things that make for a better work force, make this a better place to work, and ultimately contribute to a better job that aren't measurable by cost."

Nonetheless, the correlation is obvious. A better work force, working better, obviously is more efficient and more competitive.

But true quality circles are not designed solely to address problems of quality at the end of the line, although fully involving workers in that issue can only improve quality. Neither are they solely for workers to vent their beefs at the company.

Quality circles also set up a communication pipeline for the company to share its problems with workers on issues of profit, job security, product competition. The ability of a company to honestly and convincingly communicate and work directly with its employees on issues like those make or break a quality circle and the new communication concept.

The new relationship between employer and employee is not one of paternalism. A General Motors executive told me how he defined quality of life in the work place:

"The company is aware of the dignity of the individual and the development of the individual and that individual's work life. It's sharing. For example, you tell me all the things you like about your work. Then tell me what you don't like. If I can eliminate or minimize the things you don't like and enhance the things you do like, I will have improved your quality of work life."

I don't think that's the kind of sharing and dignity being discussed in the new-style companies. The new-style worker is looking for a much more honest and open two-way relationship with the company. He is willing to consider the good of the company because he believes in a commitment by the company to him, the worker. He is skeptical of and turned off by more "programs" to improve his workday. He is ready to be treated as an adult worker with something of value to offer the company—rather than as a child who needs to be kept pacified.

Turner thinks the quality circles at his company will take four to five years to really become a way of doing business—to evolve from a "program" status. Unfortunately, he thinks that many companies look upon the new communication with employees as simply new "programs." If economic times get a little better, many of those "programs" will go out the window.

Likewise, I believe that some smokestack companies are treating the new communication issue, with its quality circle programs, as another bone to throw only to get some desperately needed cooperation and concessions at the bargaining table. Until they honestly allow employees to work with them in the planning and organizing functions, little will change in the work areas. Those smokestack companies that will survive and evolve are only putting off that inevitable change.

Ned Huffman likens unions to children who were never properly disciplined by the company parents. The companies never took the time to tell them why the union's constant request for more candy wasn't good for them or for the company. Now the children are grown, and they have bad habits.

Most observers across the country look at unions less harshly. They reason that unions were necessary at one time; they corrected much that was wrong with the old employer-employee relationship. They did it by force because it was the only way.

But now, with the exception of a labor contract between specific workers and specific companies, some say unions have no function. Many of the general labor relations issues, like discrimination and minimum wage requirements, were championed by the original union organizers, but are now covered by federal law.

Furthermore, the unions got too big, became big business themselves. They became adversarial with companies and passed along that attitude to worker-members.

The union movement in this country was at its height in the 1930s. As early as 1964, John saw no need for a union at his factory, though he joined. He didn't change his mind when he became a supervisor and had to deal day after day with the shop steward.

John said, according to the union contract, the steward was paid his highest rate of pay when he was doing "union business." That usually meant handling a grievance of one sort or another. John said he and the union man often knew that the grievances were unfounded. Nonetheless, until the plant shutdown, the union man spent his entire forty-hour work week walking the floor, receiving his highest rate of pay from the company, handling grievances. Now, he spends about ten hours a week on union business. Even he is convinced everyone has to work harder to survive.

There are several reasons why unions are rarely found in the new-style high-tech companies. The biggest one is the combative relationship that's evolved between company and union in America.

New-style companies won't tolerate it. They specifically seek political, legal, and social climates where they can keep unions out in order to avoid the poor work attitudes and old-style work environments.

A couple of young engineers recently laid off from John Deere in Moline, Illinois, and now looking to the world of high tech, think participatory management would be impossible to achieve with unions in the picture.

"The union is counterproductive to the team because if the team is the employee and the management, where does the union fit in? As soon as the employee agrees to work as a team with management, there's no need for the union."

John agrees. When asked about participatory management, he said he wouldn't mind it if the union was sincere and paid for part of the cost of administering it. He looked upon it as purely a bargaining issue.

When I pointed out that participatory management was supposed to involve workers and management, not necessarily unions, John laughed. 'Well, workers are union. Management is company, and workers are union," he said.

Before even really considering the communication aspect, John took an adversarial position for the company firmly squared off against the union. It's a hard way to start talking seriously and working as a team.

John Gray, at the economic development group working to bring high-tech companies to Austin, says of unions: "The ethic got changed from doing the most you can to earn your money and speaking for yourself to 'Hey, man, that's not my job. I'm a carpenter, that's an electrician's job. I can't lean over to pick up a tool when it's not in my contract.'"

Everyone who has been in a union environment knows that scenario—waiting for the proper person "qualified" to touch a microphone in a television studio or a forklift in a factory. If you don't wait, you run the chance of a grievance shutting down the operation altogether.

Ted Williams, at the Research Institute in Research Triangle Park, told of this attitude from a high-tech company executive:

"If he has a piece of equipment break down, you'd have to take a Greyhound bus full of people there to repair it—a carpenter to take off the wooden guard rail, an electrician to unplug it, a plumber to disconnect the water cooling system. And they all stand back while the mechanic repairs it. Business just can't tolerate that kind of excess."

With more and more machines running in the high-tech world—from complicated test instruments to robots—one of the chief new job categories is repair technician. The technicians do it all—from diagnosing the problem to repairing it on the spot. The job is not divided into several unionized categories.

The Massachusetts High Technology Council says one of the problems with unions is the rigid structure of jobs and job titles. This doesn't fit the new high-tech environment where you might have to shift gears overnight. It's cumbersome. Unions pose similar problems when old-style industries try to adapt to new high-tech environments with new production techniques and workers in new roles.

A vocational education teacher in Florida told of an engineer friend who went to California to a unionized company where he got a good-paying job.

"As an engineer on prototype equipment, he couldn't lift a soldering iron," he said. "He had to run and get a (union) technician every time he wanted to solder something. That's not expedient when you're trying to develop something. There's always tension over that. The money was there, but as a design person, he just couldn't work like that. He came back to Florida."

The biggest reason there are few unions in new-style high-tech companies is that the companies have changed.

As Williams says: "Unions were right to correct management, but now things have swung the other way, and management has changed."

Almost everywhere I went in the new-style world of high tech, people agreed that the companies have created progressive personnel policies which make unions unnecessary.

"Most companies would rather spend the same money they would normally spend fighting unions on wages and benefits for employees," says John Gray in Austin. "They want to avoid the hassles of having to deal through a third party."

Of course, it's not all that simple everywhere. There have been relentless attempts to organize—particularly in California and Massachusetts. And it hasn't always been a pleasant battle.

David Mitchell, spokesman for the UAW, says the reason unions haven't been very successful organizing in high tech is that "it's a new industry. The job market is tight, and people are afraid. And many of the same techniques that have been employed with black briefcase union busters—fear, intimidation, and legal delays—are employed."

His final word on unions and the trend away from them: "As long as the worker doesn't have a union, he's at the mercy of management."

Mary Hammann, director of the Tucson Skill Center, in a way, echoes the union's stance: "I think management now has progressed to a point where there isn't a need for unions, but maybe it's the threat of the unions that keeps management at that point."

Randy Woods, formerly second in command in President Ford's press office, drives to work every morning down a tree-lined boulevard—a cross between an Ontario provincial park and a Caribbean island.

It takes him exactly three minutes to arrive unruffled at his glass-encased corner office overlooking a real honest-to-goodness path in the woods— well, four minutes if he misses the only street light in the area.

Randy lives and works in the Woodlands, a planned community inside the city boundaries of Houston. Many of the companies settling in the Woodlands are high-tech companies. The work place there represents an environment most high-tech companies across the country are trying to achieve.

Companies are built on large well-manicured acreages with sprawling low campus-like buildings. The pace is relaxed; the ambience informal. The beauty of the trees and lakes and architecturally pleasing buildings could lead you to think you're at a vacation resort instead of work. It's built to be a haven for thinking.

Today, new-style companies across the country build work places to serve employees. They have physical amenities like pools and indoor tracks, stylish cafeterias and sprawling parking lots. It's all part of a new-style benefits package the companies have served up voluntarily.

Most companies trying to attract the best new high-powered talent, like electrical engineers, feel they need the new work-environment package in order to compete in their national recruitment campaigns.

There are regional differences in the offerings, however. California companies are characterized as leading the fast life—Cadillac give-aways, parties, everything to meet the needs of the genius-like "Valley Boys." Supposedly, more California engineers are divorced and unsettled and looking for a fast buck in the entrepreneurial game of high tech.

Membership in the Decathalon Club, built right in the heart of Silicon Valley near Lawrence and Central Expressways, is a perk for many high-tech employees. The club is true California with babbling brooks and wooden bridges inside and tennis courts and pool outside.

But insiders say it's not a typical country club. Venture capital and talent swapping are the business topics at hand. Members usually come and go in a no-nonsense hour-long lunch. And many of the deals are cut in racquet ball courts, not over martinis.

Massachusetts companies say their employees usually are much more stable than the California variety. They're more interested in IRAs, profit sharing, and money to send their kids to college than memberships in flashy clubs.

Between the coasts, companies settling throughout the Sun Belt are including amenities from company track teams to French lessons in their new-style work places. Paradyne, a computer manufacturer in Florida, has an annual employee photo contest. The company pays for a large color print of the employee's entry into the contest. Pictures are then displayed in the company cafeteria.

Some traditional companies, like John Deere, are adopting a new-style look in their work places as well. When Deere built a new corporate headquarters facility a few years ago, it included an employee cafeteria with a decor of glass and chrome and tables grouped in a giant greenhouse that outdoes any fern bar.

As a practical matter, most high-tech companies today offer financial help for an employee's higher education—no matter at what level.

Sperry in Salt Lake City even has a program for its workers to complete high school. The classes are conducted in the plant after work hours. In the first two years, eighty people were graduated. Most of the time, Sperry says it doesn't make particularly better workers, but it makes people feel better about themselves. And it creates a good feeling toward the company.

One of the most noticeable distinctions of the high-tech work place is that dress codes and formalities give way to the entrepreneural spirit. High-tech companies tell with great pride of starting up just a few years ago with nothing but a great idea in a garage or in somebody's spare bedroom. One computer company even boasts of starting upstairs from a beauty shop. Nobody would presume to wear a necktie to work in those environments.

But as companies grow, they tend to become a bit more traditional. Stan Victor, who today could pass for a Madison Avenue ad man, told me how he watched the growth and change of the work place at Mostek in Dallas.

In the beginning (1977), he said, it was a shirt-sleeves, casual, no-necktie atmosphere. Everyone was working very hard to get the new product on line. Everyone was pulling as a team with a single purpose.

Then, an explosive growth came, and not only did everyone have to work hard and fast, but they all needed to use new skills to project an image to a market. Stan says he started wearing a tie on his own because he realized the company was a business, and he was dealing more and more with customers on the outside. Then, the dress evolved to coats and ties, and today often three-piece suits.

"We want to give our customers a feeling of stability, let them know they can deal with us for a long time," said Stan.

The change is evident internally in fast-growing companies as well. On the first day I visited Apple Computer in Cupertino, California, I passed a cubicle and saw a young man sitting at his terminal barefooted and wearing ragged cutoffs.

The next day, I noticed the same young man had "dressed." He was neatly attired in khaki slacks and topsiders. He's trying to get promoted to manager, my guide explained.

CHAPTER 4

The New Work Discipline

'They say there are only two ways to change people effectively—
brain surgery and religious conversion.''

Jerry Turner
Excello-McCord Corporation
Detroit, Michigan

'That's incorrect. Starvation will go a long way.''

Mary Hammann
Pima Skill Center
Tucson, Arizona

Just after the turn of the century when my dad was growing up in Brighton,
Iowa, his uncle Jack ran an ice business, and my dad used to help him.

Every winter, they'd go down to the Skunk River and carve out big
chunks of ice frozen on top and drag them up on the banks by horsepower.
They stored the ice in sawdust in Uncle Jack's shed. The next summer,
people in town bought the chunks to put in their ice boxes for cooling meat
and other perishables.

It was my dad's job to deliver the ice. Nobody had to explain to him how
to do his job ''right''—especially on those muggy Iowa days. If he didn't
take care of business, the product disappeared. It was the simple work ethic
of the agricultural age.

In some smokestack factories in America today a worker is paid his
highest possible rate of pay when he's not working.

It's because of the cessation rule—negotiated as part of a union contract
agreement. The intent is to cover the time when a worker is making a
transition from one task to another. It guarantees the worker top pay for up
to an hour from the time he stops working.

Needless to say, it does not make anyone rush in that hour. A worker
might go into cessation waiting for a forklift driver to move a stack of sheet
metal to his work station. Or he might be waiting for a particular tool to be
delivered to him from storage. He could spend several fifty-nine-minute
cessation periods a day.

John's job as a first line supervisor is to minimize the time in cessation and keep workers, who are paid and conditioned not to work, working and producing. It's just one of many work habits in America's smokestack industries which have become counterproductive to getting the job done—done "right." Those work habits and the adversarial relationship they create make both John and his union workers highly undesirable commodities in the new-style world of high tech.

Many new-style companies feel the old-style workers just don't fit into the new work place. They lack a quality which high-tech companies say they can't define, but can usually discern in an employment interview.

I call it a new work discipline.

It's different from the old puritan work ethic. The old ethic evolved to a point where it was dependent on guilt and negativism rather than a positive momentum. You got to work by 8:00 sharp because you had to punch the time clock. If you were just one minute late, you were punished—and you felt guilty and a little angry. You stayed until exactly quitting time because you had to punch out.

If you had a white-collar desk job without a time clock, you still stayed until 5:00, but seldom later. You became skilled at looking busy whether you were doing anything or not. If you worked in a blue-collar job, you became highly skilled not in doing your job, but in finding ways to get paid for not working.

Unions perpetuated the fall of the work ethic. They defined and categorized jobs so narrowly that workers lost sight of the work they were doing. They became more concerned with staying within the confines of their job description and with their rights to coffee breaks than with doing the job "right."

American workers are not stupid or unaware. They've watched the work ethic erode. But they've received a mixed message. In spite of the fact that many workers were sluffing off, the companies continued to be leaders in their fields. And unions, meanwhile, negotiated more and more dollars for their workers each year.

But now, smokestack industries are suffering. Many American products are deemed poorly made; unions are making wage concessions; and millions of workers are unemployed. And most important, many new-style high-tech companies don't want anything to do with the old work ethic or those who practiced it.

The new-style high-tech companies are looking for workers—hourly wage earners and managers—who are sincerely interested and involved in their work. I liken the new work discipline to the involvement in work, or labor of love, that artists have. They don't punch in and out, but they do put in long hours—and certainly not at make-work.

All the elements of the new work place are instrumental to the setting which fosters the new work discipline—communication between employer and employee, participatory management, a more relaxed atmosphere with a much less autocratic approach to getting the job done.

Workers "buy into" the job, i.e., adopt the new work discipline, only in response to a sincere and fair invitation from the company. The new work discipline results in improved quality, a pride by workers in the job they do, and less of an adversarial relationship with the company.

New-style companies begin with it as a foundation, just like communication between employer and employee.

Some old smokestack industries are trying to institute the new work discipline as part of their transition to the new-style high-technology job world. It's by far their biggest hurdle.

They start by focusing on quality—something that goes hand in hand with the new work discipline. You can only truly improve quality when it starts with the guy actually doing the work, doing the job "right." In the past, there's been little incentive for quality in the American work place. The priority passed down from top management was "get the iron out the door."

Quality has been just a department, said one high-ranking supervisor. It represented engineers—the cops—who were there because we had to have them. An inspector would come along and say, "Hey, that's not to print." They'd run to the engineer, the quality department, and argue they'd already made three hundred parts. The supervisor would want to use them because the cost goes against his budget and he's got a schedule to meet.

But this particular supervisor says that attitude is changing gradually. "Now managers have gotten together and said if we're going to survive as a division, we have to improve quality and cut costs posthaste. So now when management asks how your day is going, he doesn't want to hear how many parts you've got going out the door, he wants to hear if you've got a problem with a part that isn't quite up to snuff."

But like all the other changes in the smokestack industry, the quality issue is viewed by many employees as a flash in the pan. So, the new work discipline is slow in coming.

"Units are sitting out there unsold right now," said an engineer. "I'm sure it will revert. As soon as we don't have enough to sell out there, it will go back to the old attitude of get 'em out."

A young engineer who has worked both for an old-style smokestack company and a new-style high-tech company explained how she saw the difference in the work ethic: "At the new-style company, if we got the job done well, we could come and go as we wanted. They stressed the quality of the work, however. For example, if I did drawings, they went over them time and again for accuracy. At the old-style company, they were more interested in what colors I used on the drawings, the presentation. They were never really interested in what I was doing, just how it looked."

She said she thought new-style management and philosophy at the old-style company were just talk.

"We had a forty-five-minute movie on Japanese management, and it was fine, all philosophical, wonderful. We got back to our desks and life goes on. That was it. Nobody does anything concrete. They can shout quality, they can write quality, but there's no concrete example of when quality is going to come into play."

Another engineer agreed: "I really think you have to start with the guy making the piece, doing the work. He knows what's going on. Employees have to feel like they're doing something."

The director of human resources of a booming computer company in Colorado claims he receives some fifty or sixty phone calls a month from executives in Northeastern or Midwestern smokestack industries who want jobs.

They admit they know little about the computer business. But they insist they'll work hard to learn quickly, and will sacrifice as much as 50 percent of their six-figure salary for a chance to get out of a declining industry and into a growth industry.

The human resources director says he doesn't want them. They're too old for the new, young company—average age thirty-three. And he doesn't think they can change their old corporate ways to fit into the new work environment.

His position has a lot to do with the new work discipline. But that's hard to put into words. So, usually high-tech employers tell old-timers (forty or over) coming from old-style work places that they're "overqualified."

The prejudice against the old-style worker by high-tech companies is widespread. It extends from the blue-collar assembly line worker to the six-figure white-collar executive.

It is based on the belief that people can't change their bad habits. So despite the possible success of retraining for skills, old-style workers will still have the wrong mind-set on the job. They'll lack the new work discipline.

The prejudice surfaced blatantly in Freemont, California, where General Motors and Toyota decided to make an all-new car company with a new work place and a new kind of worker.

In March of 1982, General Motors closed two plants in California that had employed 8,909 hourly workers and 575 salaried workers.

In a matter of months there had been evictions and foreclosures, not to mention reported suicides. Dan Skrovan at General Motors was appointed head of a special retraining task force representing the company and the UAW to go to Freemont and try to help the people find new jobs. He had the aid of a UAW negotiated training fund equal to a nickel for every hour worked by a union member. Some $4 million was earmarked for the California problem immediately.

On one of Dan's first trips to California, he visited several large high-tech firms in the Silicon Valley around Freemont in an attempt to place some of GM's unemployed assembly line workers in entry-level jobs.

The high-tech firms by and large didn't want them. Dan defends his workers, and auto workers in general:

"Many of the potential employers in California have a misapprehension about what an auto assembler is. They think the assembler is the individual who has the wrench and tightens nuts on the lugs on the wheel. They think he does only physical work—just monotonous assembly.

"But they forget that all our plants have production schedules done by computer. Therefore, most of our assemblers can look at a computer printout sheet that indicates what the next car coming down the line needs—four steelbelted whitewall radials, an AM-FM stereo radio . . . it's all programmed.

"And most of the tools are pneumatic tools. Many assemblers work a panel to lift hoods, stop the line, etc. They're operating automation. Today we call it robotics.

"What I'm getting at is that our assemblers have had some smattering of computers, hydraulics, pneumatics, robotics, etc. But they're not given credit for that. They [the high-tech companies] say we don't want your assemblers. They're just manual assemblers."

But could it be the work-ethic issue at the root of the rejection? Dan says it very well could be, but it, too, is unjustified.

"A good number of our people are missing out on jobs because of preconceived notions the other employers have. Those people in Freemont all have at least fifteen years' experience. They have a company loyalty—contrary to what you might hear when they raise their dander or are provoked into some kind of labor relations issue.

"Basically, they're good employees. I would say 95 percent of the people are not the ones causing the high degree of grievances or absentee-ism. And I think it's that way in families, in schools, everywhere. It's always just a few."

In the spring of 1983, it was announced that the plant would reopen, but under a joint venture of Toyota and General Motors. Originally, the new company said it would hire three thousand workers at the plant—but offer no special consideration to the UAW workers who had previously worked the same plant.

By summer, William Usery, former U.S. labor secretary, was mediating the labor issue. Although the new company's stand was softened to welcome the old workers as the primary source of recruiting, the concept of a new-style work place was made clear:

"We're talking about building a whole new work place," said Usery, who announced the company would seek a radically different relationship with workers and their union—one based on mutual trust instead of hatred.

The plant will employ Japanese production methods, like just-in-time inventory and statistical process control. Those methods mean a lean approach dependent on quality and worker involvement and commitment.

The projected work place calls for all the elements of the new-style high-tech companies applied to an old smokestack industry. If there's a union, it will not result in an adversarial relationship with the company. Old work habits which work against productivity would be avoided. Workers are to get a bigger say in production matters and the layers of middle management are to disappear.

It's a case of a smokestack industry regrouping entirely.

Chrysler is trying that approach with its Windsor, Ontario, plant, which was closed down but reopens in the fall of 1983 as a new work place—technology in place, workers retrained, and, it is hoped, a new work discipline instilled.

Despite the high-tech apprehension, I believe American workers are capable of embracing the new work discipline. I think their decline in that area is as much the fault of rich companies as it is their representative unions for escalating excesses beyond reason.

A high-tech company executive in Texas puts it this way: "When it got out of hand in the Northeast with unions demanding $20 an hour for basically unskilled labor, management just rolled over and stopped trying to manage."

Whatever the past, America—its companies and its individuals—has only one choice today. And that is to embrace high technology in the work place—including high tech's new work environment and its new ways of working. We have no choice but to adapt.

In terms of our work, we have graduated from high school to college.

Suddenly, we're responsible for our own destinies. The rules are different. We are in an environment where we must think for ourselves. We don't ride the school bus with all the others anymore. We are free to choose where to go, to which classes, in which subjects. We are free to study or drink beer. We can take advantage of the college professor's teachings or we can sleep during class. Bells don't ring.

But the bottom line will reflect our every action. And if we faked our academics through high school or got into college on a fluke, we will fail.

In the new job market, if you come from the wrong high school, you may have a lot of trouble getting into the college you want—even as a remedial freshman. Most of the new companies are not like large state universities which can absorb all in the name of freedom of education. Work has become somewhat of a privilege, and many of the new-style high-tech companies are like elite private schools that want only their own kind.

Some—both companies and workers—may not be ready to graduate. But they will have to study extra hard for a while because classes have already begun.

Americans lost the textile industry in the 1950s, the steel industry in the 1960s, the automotive industry in the 1970s, and we'll possibly lose the electronics industry in the 1980s.

So claims Mary Hammann, director of the Tucson Skill Center, which deals with the hardcore unemployed—now including many old-style workers trying to adapt to high-tech jobs.

Mary says we're losing industries because of the high cost of producing the product, the lack of credibility in the American-made product and the lack of pride in the product by the individuals who produce it. A lot of it, she says, has to do with attitude on the job.

"I think the entire outlook of the American worker must change. I think we have to get more of the old work ethic back in. We have to identify with that product. We have to think about what we owe that particular firm. We have to ask ourselves did we earn our salary that day, not what did the company do for me.

"Employers," she says, "if they are going to be successful, cannot afford to hire for humanitarian reasons."

CHAPTER 5

Retooling America

'You can't be a D student and claim to be after high-tech jobs.''

Warren Laux
Director
Pinellas Vocational Technical Institute

Robots—the master workers of the eighties. No coffee breaks, no vacations, no sick days. Rumor has it, some even work in total darkness!

But what about those sick days? It's true robots don't get the common cold. But what happens when a hydraulic line blows or a computer chip goes bad? The fact is, robots eventually break down.

So while robots are replacing many workers doing repetitive work on the assembly line, they also have created a brand new job for people. That job is robotics technician.

Projections say that as many as twenty-five thousand to one hundred thousand robotics technicians will be working by 1990. And that's with fewer than five thousand robots working in 1983. That kind of activity in the jobs revolution is causing havoc for job hunters.

Many depressed areas, like Michigan, are grasping at the robotics technician job as a quick fix for unemployed auto workers. To an extent it makes sense. As assembly line workers are displaced by robots taking over some of their work in the plant, here's a newly created replacement job. But unfortunately, the formula isn't that simple.

For one thing, the robotics technician job requires high levels of skill—particularly in electronics, meaning that a good math background is a necessity. In Detroit alone, thousands of people are enrolled in community colleges to become robotics technicians through a UAW negotiated retraining agreement.

Many of those students, says one instructor, will never be able to do more than fill the grease bowl on the robot.

The robotics technician job is a perfect example of how the nature of work is changing dramatically with high technology.

More and more machines are doing the physical, nonthinking, repetitive work which millions of humans have been doing for years. The new jobs being created by technology are very different jobs.

Even entry-level jobs in high technology, like numeric control operator in the new-style factories or assembler in the electronics companies, require certain levels of skill. Most demand weeks of intensive training on the job.

Dan Skrovan, a training executive at General Motors for years, says we're creating new industries and jobs in high tech all right, but even the sales jobs are technical.

A recruiter from Sperry predicts that in ten years you'll be unemployable if you can't use a computer terminal. Some airlines today require even baggage handlers to be able to type twenty-five words per minute in order to communicate via a computer keyboard.

The level of technical knowledge necessary in the new job market is escalating every day.

The technician today must know about as much as the engineer was required to know just a few years ago. With the development of the microprocessor, many companies want engineers with both electrical engineering and computer science degrees. They know how to build software right into hardware.

As technical know-how becomes part of more and more job descriptions, it makes it difficult for generalists to find jobs. People who majored in liberal arts or social sciences are now losing jobs in human resources, public relations, and administration to chemists and engineers.

Technology-oriented companies like people with scientific disciplines in those positions. And often, the engineer-types don't have advanced degrees so they aren't competitive in their own job fields.

The "paper-pushers," largely middle-management generalists, are being replaced by computers that can do their jobs with the same ease and cost efficiency as the robots which are taking over the assembly line.

The routine and monotonous jobs which the industrial age offered to masses of people are diminishing. In addition to new skills, the new jobs require the ability and the willingness to think.

John's wife works in the same factory he does. She started working there in assembly years ago when they needed an extra income to make ends meet. Today she works out of habit—but in the new world of work her habits are considered bad.

"My wife is a good employee," says John. "But she'd be the first to tell you she wants no responsibility. She just works for a paycheck. But she's a good employee. She's on time, works until quitting time, and she doesn't take long breaks."

Even if John's wife retrains, acquires a new skill and becomes "involved" with her job so she practices the new work discipline, she still faces a big adjustment in the world of high tech—her paycheck.

Nearly everyone who makes the transition from the old-style job market to the new high-tech job market should be prepared for a pay cut.

New-style employers pay less and less on the low end and more and more on the high end. The rewards are for brains, not for brawn. If a machine can do your job, your salary has to reflect a saving.

Obviously, as technology advances there are fewer jobs available that more cost-efficient machines can't do. And many of those are being moved offshore where labor is very cheap. The day of the $20-an-hour blue-collar worker is coming to an end.

At the same time, machines don't have the ideas that create the new products or the entrepreneurial spirit that the top engineering talent does. So, most high-technology companies are constantly recruiting top talent with very high price tags.

Many companies offer bounties to their present engineering staff for finding a "talent" that will leave another company and go to work with them. The practice started in Silicon Valley, where reportedly the engineering commodities hop from job to job for the dollar with great regularity.

Today companies throughout the Sun Belt offer as much as $2,000 cash to the employee who recruits another.

Average-size high-tech companies report that with or without bounties they spend as much as $8,000 to $10,000 just to recruit a single middle-level engineer.

On the other end of the spectrum, if you're like John's wife with no particular skills, plan on starting at an entry-level job that will pay as low as $4.50 an hour.

From a dollar point of view, the high-tech job market presents a polarized picture—very low paid, low skilled workers at one end and very high paid, highly skilled workers at the other. There are few jobs left in the middle with relatively high pay and relatively low skills. Until now, the masses worked in those jobs. The jobs were their ticket to the middle class.

Training, or retooling our labor force, is what many see as the key to surviving the social byproducts of our changing job market. But it's a very complex task. First we must retrain workers in new skills. Then we must address the new work discipline, their attitude toward their work. We must address the problems of pay—determine how to help a worker making $25,000 a year learn to live on $12,000. And finally, we must deal with the technophobiacs who simply don't want to evolve to the age of technology.

A lot of people—blue collar and white collar—are just plain scared of it. A recruiter at Sperry says he sees it every day:

"I think there's this subtle intimidation of a high-tech job whether it's in computers or whatever. Certainly, there's a lot of high technology in the auto industry, but for the average line worker there's an intimidation which I think is unfounded. They're just not sure what they're going up against. They wonder, can I really hack something like this?

"I don't think they understand that what we do at a very basic level is really just an assembly approach. We work with something a little more delicate, a little more defined than the mass production of machinery. But they're afraid they'll get laughed out of here because they don't know what we do.''

And it's not just entry-level assemblers who suffer from technophobia.

"Even students in technical curriculums and in engineering and computer science in college don't fully appreciate what goes on here. They give this real sigh of relief when they get on the job and realize they don't have to come in and know everything, sit down from day one and start producing.''

"The adjustment is cultural. It isn't governmental; it is somewhat educational; but it's mostly cultural,'' says Ed Beck, a training adviser in the U.S. Treasury Department.

"The transition is happening right now as kids are playing with Atari games or programming a microwave oven. My twelve-year-old is learning how to program, and he can actually program simple programs into the computer. He can generate simple games. He's reading everything he can get his hands on. He's going to be prepared for changes that are coming. He may never be a programmer, but he'll be computer smart. He's making the transition from an industrial to a technological society.''

There's a major awareness gap about what's happening in this country, he says. Unfortunately, too many people are trying to fix it with a Band-aid approach.

The robotics technician situation is an example of desperate people trying to patch up a deep-seated revolutionary jobs problem with a Band-aid. In the Detroit area, one community college alone has three thousand students enrolled to become robotics technicians. The numbers have gotten so outrageous that the Upjohn Institute for Employment Research in Kalamazoo, Michigan, predicted in early 1983 that already we were producing too many robotics technicians for our needs—before anyone had even graduated from a two-year course.

The robotics technician job also illustrates another major problem with retraining. There is a tremendous lack of understanding and information about the jobs we are retraining people to fill.

In Michigan, if you train to become a robotics technician, the job is perceived to be similar to a skilled tradesman, like a maintenance electrician. In fact, many who are being retrained there are electricians with ten to fifteen years' experience. Theoretically, as robotics technicians, they'll go back to work in the auto plants, servicing the new equipment, the robots.

But out west and in the Sun Belt, there's a different perception of the job.

Schools like Red Rocks Community College in Denver view the job as a service representative troubleshooting for the robot manufacturer in the field. Traditionally, he's the guy who wears a shirt and tie on the job and carries his tools in his briefcase. (There are a few women training to be robotics and other technicians, I might add. But by and large, it's still a man's world.)

State and national task forces are working feverishly to settle on a standardized job profile and training curriculum for the robotics technician and other jobs. But it's easy to see that retraining is difficult when you don't know exactly what the new jobs are.

Jerry Forrest, a consultant working on job standardization for the Michigan Department of Education, says when you train for a new high-tech job, you need to be flexible. Things change so fast that a graduate of high-tech training can usually count on a job staying the same no more than two years.

That puts a strain on schools as well as people trying to stay current. Pinellas Vocational Technical Institute, a successful high-tech training institution in Florida, has a course of study for electro-mechanical technician which is basically a forerunner to a robotics course. One of the teachers told me some schools in the country have a similarly titled course that trains students to fix appliances like dishwashers.

Finally, high-tech companies themselves add to the confusion. There's little standardization of job title or job description from one company to another.

An electronics technician, for example, at one company might do something totally different from an electronics technician at another company. Most companies also have preferred schools, especially for job areas like technician.

That's led to a national movement to coordinate local training courses to cater to local industry's needs. In fact, that's the theory of the federal government's new Job Partnership Training Act. The theory is good in areas where high tech has settled and growth is forecast.

Mary Hammann at the Tucson Skill Center says: "Our training areas change as rapidly as our local labor market changes. Industry almost runs this place with the exception of telling us how to teach. Industry tells us what equipment to buy, what standards to train for, and what the new techniques and standards are."

In the twenty years of the school's existence, she says only the Business and Office course has kept the same name in the curriculum guide. And, with automated office machines, it bears little resemblance to the old course.

She says high-tech employers tend to drop their prejudice against old-style workers if they've been trained under the company's watchful eye.

In San Antonio, a voluntary industrial council is being formed which will send volunteers from industry to the high schools twice a month to try to compensate in part for a lack of good math and science teachers.

Dallas also has a school-business partnership in which local businesses send representatives to sit on the school board.

Obviously, the established high-tech growth areas can utilize the community involvement education approach well. But what about the old Northeastern and Midwestern communities where the only community businesses they can look to for guidance are old-style smokestack industries which haven't made the transition to high tech and new ways of working themselves. Furthermore, they aren't hiring.

The question we must ask as a nation is if electronics technicians are trained in Muncie, with local industry input, who will hire them?

As a country, we are in trouble because our levels of basic education are declining just when we need better educated workers.

Millions and millions of people need retraining, says a trainer at Sperry. We have never had to deal with a problem of this magnitude before, but we must recognize it as a fact of life.

If there were any doubts about it, the National Commission on Excellence in Education released an open letter to the American people in the spring of 1983 that couldn't have been more blunt.

"What was unimaginable a generation ago has begun to occur. Others are matching and surpassing our educational attainments. If an unfriendly power had attempted to impose on America the mediocre educational performance that exists today, we might well have viewed it as an act of war," says the letter.

That view is very similar to our reaction to the industrialization of others and their competition with our old smokestack industries. But we have to face the fact that our educational system got lazy just like our big smokestack industrial powers.

The commission reported that 23 million American adults are functionally illiterate by the simplest tests of everyday reading, writing, and comprehension.

Some 13 percent of all seventeen-year-olds can be considered functionally illiterate—it's as high as 40 percent among minority youth.

Most standardized tests show a steady decline in achievement levels of our high school graduates over the last twenty-five years.

Even engineers on the job for years lack some of the basic skills of communication, an obvious failure somewhere in our educational system.

Susan Crissman, a consultant at Apple Computer, worked through Stanford University a couple of years ago tutoring engineers on the job in how to write.

Susan says there's no relationship whatsoever between your brilliance in your engineering field and how well you can write.

The approach to the Stanford writing course was different from many. It was based on the fact that even if all the red marks were corrected on many high school essays, the paper still wouldn't be an "A" paper. Usually, the paper didn't say anything in the first place.

So, Susan started her writing course by asking the engineers a very basic question: What are you trying to say and to whom? "Those things usually never cross an engineer's mind," said Susan.

The decline of educational standards in the United States has gone hand-in-hand with simple needs for industrial workers to do monotonous, nonthinking jobs year after year.

Mary Hammann tells about a Tucson Skill Center pilot program for some of the ten thousand laid-off area copper workers.

They came in with a lot of hostility. They felt isolated. They had tried to tap into public services for assistance. Some found they didn't qualify. Others were simply not experienced enough with the system to understand how to use it.

They had untransferrable skills. So retraining was a necessity to fit into the growing high-tech industries in Tucson. But the big problem was salary.

"The copper workers were making $15 an hour," said Mary. "I looked at their skill level, and it was so sad. The hardest part was, they sincerely believed they were worth $15 an hour. But the education level, the skill level, just wasn't there—they could make $3.65 an hour once they'd gone through a retraining assembly program."

Nonetheless, fewer than 1 percent left the Skill Center because they knew it was their last hope. After they retrained and accepted the job for $3.65 an hour, the real shock for most was when they realized that in ten years they could only increase to $5 an hour if they didn't train further for a more technical job.

Mary believes that along with training for new jobs, the Skill Center must help people to adjust to a new style of living, with the aid of mental health counselors and whatever else it takes.

And with all that, if you ask Mary about the work discipline and how you change the mindset of the old-style worker, she replies:

"You can't. I think you have to lay it out the way it is and open the doors. They have to be willing to walk through."

At Pinellas Technical Vocational Institute in Florida, a course to orient old-style workers to the new-style work place, including responsibility in the more free structure, is required of every graduate.

If students are late for class or don't show up, they get "fired." They are thrown out of the course and must enroll again the next quarter.

"You try to explain to a student, if you're late here, you'll be late on the job. If you goof off here, you'll goof off on the job," said a teacher.

The buzz word for the eighties is retraining.

Money and facilities are going into massive retraining efforts at each of the big automakers to equip workers—employed and unemployed—with skills needed in a world of high-technology manufacturing.

Vocational schools and community colleges have never been more popular or held in higher esteem.

Response, if nothing more than rhetoric, has been quick in coming to the acknowledged crisis in our nation's school systems.

But Dan Skrovan at General Motors warns that the national condition is spawning its share of rip-off retraining schemes geared to desperate people who think they can buy back into the job market.

The most common quickie schemes are what Dan calls the One Hour Overview . . . of Robotics, of Computers, etc. Such courses are prevalent particularly in high unemployment areas in the Northeast and Midwest.

But you can't prepare for a job in the high-tech world with a quickie overview of anything. The auto industry, for instance, is looking primarily at specific training for the short term—supplying somebody quickly to operate a particular new machine. And to get the basics of any useful technology today usually requires at least two years of school.

Targeting a job (explained later) really begins with training. If you're getting ready to enroll in five years of engineering, you should try to go to a good school near the geographic area you think you want to work when you graduate.

Aside from the very top-rated Stanford University in Palo Alto, California, and Massachusetts Institute of Technology in Boston, companies usually recruit new engineering and science graduates from colleges in their part of the country.

If you're looking for training in a vocational school or community college, there are a number of pertinent questions you should consider before enrolling:

• Decide where you want to live when you graduate and go to work. Then target several companies in that area and make sure they hire for the job for which you're training.

• Call the human resources offices and ask whether the company has preferred schools.

• If you don't know any companies in the area, ask the school whether it has an industrial council (most good ones do) and who's on it. You're not asking for a promise of a job, just an idea of where you might look when you graduate.

• Be sure you understand the recommended prerequisites, particularly in math and science, for your selected course of study. You're doomed to fail the course, let alone get a job, if you don't have the basics under your belt.

• Ask the school to give you a profile of the job or jobs for which you should be prepared when you graduate. Be sure that profile matches the image you have.

• Many high-tech companies offer extensive in-house training today in order to keep up with their technical staff needs and to train people to work particularly the company way. Don't overlook the possibility of starting in a low-level, low-skilled job with the company and taking advantage of those programs. It can be a big money saver—a way to earn while you learn.

CHAPTER **6**

Jobs Mom Didn't Tell You About

"My mother still wants to know what I do here.
Semiconductors? What's that, she asks."

> Sheila Sandow
> Semiconductor Industry Association
> Cupertino, California

I was in junior high school when I announced one night at the dinner table that I had decided to be a journalist. My parents agreed that was fine— knowing that teen-age whims come and go.

But when I enrolled in the University of Iowa School of Journalism, my dad stepped in. If we were to invest in four years of higher education, I ought to come out with at least a teaching certificate—something to "fall back on."

Well, fifteen years later, few fathers would repeat that advice.

Today, only about 50 percent of teaching graduates go to work teaching, compared to the more than 70 percent when I graduated from college in the late 1960s. Declining birthrates are responsible primarily. The one exception is a growing demand for secondary-grade math and science teachers. Many who train in those areas get more attractive offers to work in private industry than in the classroom, so school systems seem to always have openings.

But I'm not blaming Dad for his advice. Fifteen years ago teaching was considered as secure a job as one with the federal government. But then, federal government jobs aren't what they used to be either. Teaching was an especially good job for a woman. She could teach a few years, take off and have a family, and then return if and when she wanted to after the kids were grown.

Needless to say, there've been plenty of changes, not the least of which was a record-breaking number of women entering "men's jobs" in the 1970s. Today women can be comfortable pursuing almost any job that a man can, and in more and more homes, parenting has become a shared responsibility. So, if Mom has been a less informed job adviser in the past, she certainly can speak with authority now.

But there's another reason for the Jobs Mom Didn't Tell You About— aside from Mom's lack of worldliness. The jobs may not have existed five years ago.

Technology is undeniably the catalyst for a lot of new jobs. We couldn't have had data processors, for instance, before technology brought us the computer. We certainly couldn't have robotics technicians without robots. It seems new jobs are being created overnight to keep pace with the technological changes in our work place.

So, what do today's parents, moms and dads, tell their kids to be when they grow up? Better yet, what do Mom and Dad do about keeping up and keeping a job?

My advice, and the advice of many others, is that you must be flexible. Maybe you study or train in a course called Robotics Technician. But be prepared to apply the basic knowledge you learn about hydraulics, electronics, and our automated world in a variety of ways.

It's like learning how to fly an airplane. You get a private pilot's license when you have mastered the basics of flying—aerodynamics, weather, navigation, maneuvers like landing and taking off. Later, you get checked out or rated in various types of aircraft.

For example, you may learn how to fly in a 150-horsepower single engine, two-seater. But later you could apply the same basics to get checked out in a jet.

The same concept of basics applies in the new technical job market. The difference is in 1983, less than one-third of 1 percent of Americans were licensed to fly airplanes. And in the new job market, the number of people needing some degree of technical skill to work will approach 100 percent.

My advice also is, if it is technical, it's probably a good job choice at least until the end of this century. That's not to say, however, that what's state-of-the-art today will be so tomorrow.

But, in general, if you want to be a secretary, try to learn word processing and other skills used in electronic offices. Don't depend on the old standbys—typing and shorthand. If you take training before you get a job, get the best broad training in an automated office environment using a variety of equipment. Then when you target a particular company, try to brush up on its particular system of equipment and software.

If you're destined for something blue collarish, be sure you can function on an automated line. Plan on a job as an operator of machinery rather than as a physical laborer. You'll need basic skills like reading, writing, and possibly typing (for keyboarding computers). You can usually pick up the specifics of operating particular machinery on the job.

Technician may well become the largest job classification of the twenty-first century. Technicians with all kinds of specialties are becoming truly the backbone of the world of technology—playing instrumental roles in manufacturing and in repairing our automated world. Technicians generally work in some capacity between creation and production in manufacturing or as assistants to professionals in research and development and service areas.

Of course, the **engineer** is definitely a top-rated professional slot for the 1980s. From fall 1981 to fall 1982, private industry hired seven thousand new engineers. There are twenty-five different engineering specialties, but the areas of **chemical, civil, electrical/electronics, industrial,** and **mechanical** seem to have the most new jobs. Practically every high-tech firm and firm going high tech is in the market for certain engineers—not to mention federal, state, and local governments. Even when "applications are not being taken," a good engineer can usually count on at least an interview.

It may be easier to understand what new jobs are if you understand the new technology where the work is being done.

The majority of new jobs are in the field of electronics—a vast field with many specialties responsible for most of the new industries we call high tech today. The industries are moving and developing so fast that there are few good sources for national statistics.

The American Electronics Association, with two thousand member companies, seems to be the best group keeping tabs on growth and jobs. It estimates that there are eleven thousand known electronics-associated firms in business today. They have 3.7 million people working. The association does a yearly benchmark wage and salary report for electronics job categories, designed to be an industry guide.

Here are some of the major categories of business within the electronics industry:

Computer Manufacturers. IBM, Hewlett-Packard, Apple are among the most recognizable companies. They design and build computers, ranging from the rather simple personal computers to the massive main frames that handle information to run the big enterprises like the government.

Software Firms. Software specialists design the programs to actually perform tasks using the logic in the computer. The field is booming as an industry separate from computer manufacturers because things are happening so fast the computer makers don't always have time to build both better hardware and software.

Peripheral Manufacturers. They make the accessories for computers—everything from expanded memory storage devices to printers.

Semiconductor Manufacturers. The "chipmakers" design and produce the tiny silicon chips with electronic circuitry that operate everything from computers to automobiles in our high-tech world.

Electronic Component Companies. These companies produce the minute parts, like transistors and diodes, that integrate the information on printed circuit boards.

Telecommunications Companies. These futuristic companies—ranging from American Bell to cable television companies—are finding new ways to transmit information by voice, print, and video within offices and through space.

Consumer Electronics Companies. They make video games and video recorders primarily.

Defense Contractors. These firms work with high levels of security under government contracts to do anything from designing a secret communications antenna system to building the MX missile.

Biomedical Manufacturers. Electronics in medicine is used in artificial organs and limbs and in complicated test equipment and systems.

Industrial Equipment Manufacturers. Robotics is the chief application of electronics in the industrial world. Robots are manufactured and sold to work not only in old smokestack industries but in many high-tech electronics industries as well.

There are three key jobs common to most areas of electronics—**assembler, electronics technician,** and **electronics engineer.**

The **assembler** can be an entry-level job, but once you get in, there are many variations of the job—all of which are promoted from within. It is a skilled job, but usually the company will train you even at the entry level. Pay is low to start—in a range from about $4 an hour to $8 or $9 an hour.

Unlike an old-style assembly line worker, sometimes called assembler also, the new-style assembler's job is much less physical. Assemblers usually don't drill holes, or attach big parts to a big product, like a bumper to a car.

Rather, they work at a bench or work station with very small electronic parts or components. The most common beginning assembly job is soldering tiny parts to a printed circuit board. Assemblers work from a set of written directions for the assembly, usually an electronic schematic. Most companies say the only skill a person needs to have to be an assembler is manual dexterity. In-house training for the job runs at least several weeks.

The assembler job can be very tedious. The vast majority of assemblers are women, perhaps representing second family incomes that can tolerate the low pay.

Some assemblers move on to higher level and higher paying jobs as assemblers working in test and automated assembly functions.

A woman working today as a test supervisor at Paradyne in Florida told me proudly that she started there better than eleven years ago as an assembler, but stayed in that position only one week.

Assembler jobs are available at computer manufacturers, peripheral manufacturers, consumer electronics companies, and medical manufacturers, among others. In Colorado there are even some cottage industries which hire assemblers for printed circuit board work subcontracted from larger companies.

However, the assembler's job is becoming more and more automated. Many companies now use a wave soldering process in which printed boards with components in place are skimmed through a hot bath of solder on a conveyor belt. Automated systems also are in place in several companies to select and place the various components on the boards before soldering. The people who run the machines, however, generally still are called assemblers.

Electronics technicians are in demand in almost every area of the electronics industry, but the job can vary tremendously from one business group to another and even from company to company. Most companies are very selective about how their electronics technicians are trained. Most have preferred schools, and many run in-house training courses in order to establish the "company way" of doing things.

In general, you need at least a two-year vocational course in order to get this job. However, when businesses are growing rapidly and can't get enough technicians, they often train an assembler who shows the talent and interest.

The duties of the job include:

• Actually building electronics subassemblies for prototype models.

• Calibrating electronic instruments.

• Troubleshooting an electronics system to find the cause of a malfunction.

• Conducting routine engineering tests or detailed experimental tests.

• Solving mechanical or electronic problems in new products.

The electronics technician works closely with the engineer—usually as part of a project team. A technician's duties can become very, very specific once on the job. One technician working at a Colorado aerospace company, for instance, was charged with programming a robot to solder components on a giant defense antenna.

Electronics technicians must have a good understanding of practical electronic theory. From there, they might also become computer repairmen, robotics technicians, or with lots of experience, the higher skilled "super techs." Super technicians work in research and development with design engineers and utilize basic engineering principles with their electronics background. The World Future Society predicts there will be jobs for 1.1 million electronics technicians by 1990.

Electronics engineers, or "double E's" as they're called, are the hot commodities in the electronics business. The ones with advanced degrees and years of experience—and creative minds—are the entrepreneurs who invent new products and start companies in their garages or spare bedrooms. They're the ones who are wooed from company to company as the thinking talent necessary today in the highly competitive product race.

Many of them become management. Pay for the best can go to six figures. Many double E's become millionaires with good profit-sharing plans in the companies they start or join on the ground floor.

At the entry level, most good bachelor's degree graduates have a choice of jobs. In fact, the American Electronics Association predicts that industry demands for engineering graduates will be twenty-three thousand greater than supply annually through 1985.

Electronics engineers actually design the new products—from computers to electronic games to electronic parts on spaceships. By definition, the job title electronics engineer is almost interchangeable with electrical engineer.

If you still wish Mom would just let you move back in rather than continuing your exploration of the changing job world, maybe a walk through a couple of basic industries will help. I'll point out the people working—tell you what they're called and what they're doing.

The foundation industries in the world of electronics are semiconductors and computers. They're being combined as well into microelectronics, which, in essence, is putting computers on tiny semiconductor chips.

THE CHIPMAKERS

Silicon is the source. It's a very durable natural substance found in sand. There are companies today that grow silicon from crystals in laboratories into long, round sausage-like forms. Then they slice the "sausages" into ultra-thin "wafers." A wafer might average four inches in diameter. Semiconductor manufacturers can get as many as five hundred individual silicon "chips" on a single wafer.

The making of semiconductor chips starts with the development of the intricate electronic circuits to go on each chip. That's done, of course, by computers and the commonly known computer aided design (CAD) system.

Electronics engineers design the circuitry that performs the marvels of electronics for us in our cars, dishwashers, and spaceships or that simply files volumes of information.

Electronics technicians work with the engineers. Usually, the design work is done in a quiet area near the administrative section of the company. Engineers and technicians work in cubicle offices where they can easily gather and compare notes whenever they need to.

When a design is ready to be tested or produced on a chip, a **computer draftsman** translates the engineer's notes into a digital code which a **computer automated** (or **aided**) **design operator** keyboards into the computer system.

Then, the magic begins. A giant roll of drafting paper is threaded into the

CAD machine and the digital information entered is translated so that a plotter actually draws hard copies of precise circuitry blueprints.

Once the circuit designs are tested and proven ready for actual production, we move into the chips production area—called the wafer fabrication, or front-end area.

When the blank wafers come in, they are first coated with a material that's light sensitive, a material similar to an emulsion on a film. **Entry-level** or **basic operators** perform this task. They must dress in clean room garb and work in rooms lighted only by yellow light. The wafer photo process filters out yellow light just as many photo darkrooms filter out red light and thus are lighted only by red. ·

After coating the wafers, the operators must bake them in ovens to harden the surface.

After baking, operators imprint the complex circuit designs onto the wafers by a variety of processes, each similar to a photo printing process. The huge design, as it comes out of the CAD department on a sheet of paper sometimes two by three feet, is shrunk to chip size, about a quarter the size of an average fingernail.

The operator follows the printing process by an etching process, sometimes using a laser. The chip is then "developed" by dipping it into an acid solution which eats away parts of the chips exposed to light, leaving tiny troughs where the circuitry runs.

There are usually several layers of circuitry on each chip, so the entire process must be repeated for each layer. It's important, however, each time a layer is added that it be properly aligned with the adjoining layer so that the circuits will interact properly. Ions are actually implanted by another machine in the fabrication area to connect the three-dimensional circuitry.

The alignment job is done using a machine, employing a microscope to see the minute areas, but it must be actually accomplished by a human, in this case it's again an operator.

There are no schools to learn the skills of wafer fab operators. Most companies hire operators with good reading and writing skills and give them intensive on-the-job training. Operators often start on the aligner machines and move up to more complicated tasks like operating the furnaces to bake the wafers.

Lead operators supervise a particular work area and are akin to first line supervisors in a factory.

Also in the fab area, as it's called, are technicians. They keep the highly precise machinery running. One major semiconductor manufacturer calls them **R&M technicians**, repair and maintenance technicians.

If lasers are used, **laser technicians** are needed as well.

These technicians, like electronics technicians, need a minimum of two years' training in a vocational course.

Chemical and **manufacturing** or **process engineers** work in the fab areas too. They oversee the delicate production process, including finely adjusting the machinery to create precise tolerances. They're followed by another engineering team constantly trying to improve the chips, making them smaller with faster circuitry.

In the last few years, semiconductor companies have been accused of singlemindedly pursuing faster and smaller chips, disregarding their end market and its real needs. There were good reasons for that singlemindedness.

Obviously, if you can make a chip smaller, you can get more of them on each wafer at no additional cost.

And just by nature of being smaller, it's faster—the current has less distance to flow through smaller circuitry—and thus, makes response time to our pushing buttons better. Smaller, faster chips also use less electricity and build up less heat, a contributor to electronic failures.

But recently, particularly with the economic downturn of 1982 and 1983 which affected the semiconductor industries about the worst of any of the high-tech industries, the companies have had to become much more market-oriented. They must find a buyer for a custom chip, get his specifications, and be ready to produce it in a given period of time within a budget. That has resulted in a new-found demand for good marketing personnel at semiconductor companies. But again, they must be technically oriented in order to know their product and strategize its use and sale.

When the wafers come out of the fab area, they go to testing where more operators and **testers** monitor mostly an automated process.

A machine puts an electrical charge through the wafer to test each chip's circuitry. Any chip which doesn't work properly gets a drop of red dye automatically. Some companies sort the chips according to their speed at this point as well. (Faster chips bring a higher price.)

After the testing and sorting, the wafer is carefully cut into individual chips by an automated diamond tip saw. The red dot chips are discarded, and the good ones go to the next area, assembly.

The assembly area is an extremely labor-intensive area which inevitably will be totally automated. **Assemblers** package the chips into little plastic or ceramic containers which must be tediously wired into the chip in order to transmit the circuitry to the ultimate printed circuit board where the chip will function.

Almost all assembly is now being done in offshore locations because labor is cheap and transportation of the lightweight, minuscule parts is not a big factor.

THE COMPUTER BUILDERS

The other major new industry Mom probably told you little if anything about is computers. The first computer was built only forty years ago at the University of Pennsylvania. It took machinery that would fill up your finished basement to perform the simplest logic tasks.

The growth of the industry has been measured in shrinkage. Today, computers much more complex than that first one can be built on a tiny silicon chip a quarter the size of your fingernail. The applications for computers have been unlimited—from running offices to spaceships.

Most of the major companies agree that computers are built by people working in teams, usually called project teams.

The process starts with the design team, a research and development group made up of **development engineers, computer science specialists,** and **electronics technicians**. The design team, usually five to twenty people, identifies new products and decides how to build and manufacture them.

Each member of the team has a specialty to contribute to the overall building of the computer. An **electrical engineer** is one of the primary designers dealing with the electronic design that will make the computer run. Often the project, or team, leader is an electrical engineer.

Others on the team are **software specialists, process** and **mechanical engineers,** and **systems engineers**.

The technicians need at least a two-year associate's degree in addition to experience as demanded by their role on the team. The professionals on the design team need a degree in engineering, computer science, or a related scientific discipline like physics.

The team works closely together to make certain that the entire system will work. They work individually, possibly with technicians or engineering aides, to solve the problems of their specific specialty.

A design team can work on a new product for several years.

The job of the prototype team overlaps that of the design team. As the name implies, this team actually builds the computer, and rebuilds and rebuilds it until the "bugs" are worked out. **Manufacturing engineers** and **product assurance** or **quality assurance engineers** are key team members.

The quality engineers test for problems with overheating—always a potential problem with electronics—and make sure the software that operates the computer functions properly.

The prototype team uses a variety of people who do the actual building from **electronics technicians** to **assemblers** to **inventory control specialists** and **materials specialists**.

Some companies hire these people on a temporary basis from contract labor agencies.

The computer industry is moving so fast and is so competitive that once a product is conceived by the design team, marketing begins. So, prototypes often are built under a lot of pressure on a very tight schedule in order to get into mass production and fill back orders.

The manufacturing team brings the computer product from the prototype stage to mass production. The team develops and institutes the best production methods to assure product quality, productivity, and profit.

Electrical, mechanical, and **industrial engineers** are among key team members. They work closely with **electronics technicians** and **production technicians** to implement their manufacturing concepts.

Assemblers do the actual mechanical assembly of computers—everything from fitting together housings to soldering tiny components on printed circuit boards. Assemblers also perform tests on many electronic parts as well as the complete product to assure reliability.

Much of the assembly function is becoming automated, but companies generally still need assemblers or operators to monitor the equipment. Most testing today is done by at least a semiautomated process.

Computer firms buy a variety of components for their product lines from outside vendors. For example, some firms may build and assemble their own printed circuit boards while others may purchase them. Almost all computer companies buy their power supplies and housing assemblies from outside vendors. Some even buy custom-designed integrated circuits.

The purchasing function for technical parts has opened up a booming career field in materials management. **Materials engineers, materials technicians,** and **buyers** all work to determine the reliability and usability of parts while maintaining the best quality at the best price.

They are extremely technical jobs and because of the large costs involved are as important to the end product as the people on the project teams.

Because of the many parts that go into a computer and the complexity of building it, the industry also uses **inventory control specialists** who make sure the right materials are there at the right time in the manufacturing process.

People with degrees in business (often a master's in business administration) and others with degrees in mechanical, electrical, or quality engineering fill slots in materials management.

Marketing in the computer industry demands the very best marketing skills because of the extreme competition among products and companies. And it requires a high level of technical knowledge in order to understand how to compare products and identify advantages and disadvantages of each.

Job titles range from **marketing engineer** (someone with a degree in engineering and a master's degree in business) to **field sales representative** and **systems representative** (a minimum of a bachelor's degree, preferably in a scientific discipline) to **applications engineer** (minimum degree in engineering).

Whether you're selling a major computerized data system to a large commercial client or a personal computer to an individual at a retail computer store, the marketing department of the manufacturer is responsible for helping the end user make best use of the product.

For commercial sales, systems representatives work directly with buyers to custom design computer systems to best satisfy that company's needs. For retail sales of personal computers, **customer support specialists** develop in-store demonstration programs, training classes, write customer manuals, etc.

Jobs created by the computer go far beyond the manufacturer of the machine. There's an entire industry of technicians who install and repair computers. They may work for the manufacturer, the retailer, or for themselves as dealer authorized repairmen.

The sales staffs at retail computer stores are not exactly shoe salesmen. They must be computer smart—smart enough to demonstrate products, compare technical points, and match up what you want to do with your computer to the capabilities of various software packages.

And that introduces an entirely separate industry spawned by computers—the software industry. A computer by itself has a certain logic built into it. But it cannot perform specific tasks unless it has certain instructions, or sets of rules called software programs. Computer companies often subcontract with other companies to develop or "write" the software programs.

Electrical engineers with software as a specialty and **programmers** make up the nucleus of employees in software companies.

Finally, along with computers, we have developed needs for printers to make copies of information on paper or hard copies, storage devices like magnetic disks to keep files of information, modems to hook up to other computers by telephone, and a host of other "peripheral devices." Again, the computer manufacturers make some of their own peripherals, but the growth and diversity of the computer industry has made it possible for many companies to open strictly to supply a peripheral product.

THE NEW MANUFACTURERS

Computers have changed many old manufacturing industries into much different places to work. They've replaced some old-style workers and created new jobs for others.

The old smokestack industries have just begun to be revolutionized by computers. But already many factories barely resemble factories as they were five years ago. As a Washington, D.C., observer puts it: "There aren't any people there anymore!"

A trip to Coors Brewery in Golden, Colorado, is like a trip on the Enterprise. At one point in the production process, giant vats of "brew" stand as though abandoned in a spotless room the size of half a football field. A single operator works in a well-ventilated, glassed-in room which overlooks the vats. Panels of lights fill the back wall and stand in multiple rows of waist-high consoles. They are indicators for computers which control the precise temperatures, formulas, and timing of the brewing process. The operator's job is simply to monitor the digital readouts for the variables and watch for flashing warning lights indicating an imbalance.

Coors approaches the "Factory of the Future," which computerized factory automation systems could create. In the totally automated factory, the lights could be turned out because no one would work on the factory floor—no one that is except the robots.

The manufacturing process would begin with the design of new products. Engineers would sit before a computer terminal with a very special electronic sketch pad. As they roughed out new products, the computer would automatically translate the sketch into a finished design, precisely to specifications.

Basic CAD operators would run various software programs to test the designs for practical use.

After engineering modifications, the design information would automatically and electronically be transferred to automated production equipment on the factory floor. A production order would be programmed into the CAM (computer aided manufacturing) system, and the assembly line would roll.

Some robots would build the product while others with vision and other sensory attributes would maintain the highest quality standards by performing computerized inspection of parts and product during the manufacturing process.

Computer programmers and **manufacturing** or **process engineers** would constantly strive for improved systems of manufacturing.

The **systems engineer** would be among the highest level jobs in the factory. He would be the one to know the total automated system, understand how everything ties together, order the higher level software, and troubleshoot breakdowns.

Highly skilled **maintenance** and **repair technicians**, with a vast knowledge of electronics and hydraulics or pneumatics, would keep the equipment running.

It may sound far-fetched, but very reputable and successful companies, like General Electric, are busy today building the technology to make it happen. And, in fact, factories much like the one described are operating already in Japan.

In the meantime, the American smokestack factory job market is in total chaos.

Technology is making its way to industries like automobile manufacturing. In several instances, entire plants have been shut down, renovated, and reopened with retrained workers. But company spokesmen insist the new jobs are just upgraded versions of old jobs.

They're keeping the same job titles, but adopting new skills and duties. Machinists are doing the job of programmers. Electricians are becoming robotics technicians. Assembly line workers are becoming numeric control operators.

Although we're headed that way, in reality, the pure Factory of the Future isn't running in American today.

In the CAD system, for instance, design engineers still use pencils to draw roughs on old-fashioned paper pads. The **computer draftsman** then translates the design to a form which the **digitizing equipment operator** can enter into the CAD system. Both hard copy precision drawings and a numeric control tape come out of the CAD system.

The tape is hand-carried to the factory where it's fed by the **numeric control operator** into single-function automated machinery.

Robots, at a minimum, are welding, painting, and assembling major automobile parts. **Robotics technicians** are being trained to at least maintain the robot, if not diagnose malfunctions.

It's hard to predict the speed of job changes in American manufacturing plants. Unions are a major factor. They certainly won't stand by quietly while thousands more of their workers are shifted out the door.

But the change in manufacturing, say many, is inevitable if American smokestack companies are to compete in the technological global marketplace.

THE ELECTRONIC OFFICE

The "electronic office," equipped with computers and telecommunications systems, is a dramatic example of the impact of "information age" technology in the work place. Secretary, clerk, and receptionist jobs are changing into a host of new jobs like **word processor, data processor,** and **information specialist.**

Some of the change is gradual. The secretary stays a secretary; a word processor simply replaces her typewriter. But all of a sudden, her ability to get out fifty perfectly typed letters in record time is of no value. The computer's form letter software can accomplish the same task in a fraction of the time. The secretary's old ability is obsolete, and furthermore, perhaps after years on the job, she must learn a new skill—operating the computer.

The theory behind the true electronic office is that individual managers do not need separate secretaries in the traditional sense. Rather, they share the services of a pool, often called the administrative support center.

The specialists who work in the pool are either data entry specialists or word processing specialists. They work all day sitting in front of a terminal screen which electronically hooks them to the company's data base of information—everything they may need from payroll records to technical research reports to correspondence. They talk to co-workers by "electronic mail"—by typing messages on their keyboard to be read by others on their desktop terminal screens. It's the simplest example of telecommunications at work.

When support specialists arrive in the morning, they "log on" by typing their individual codes into the terminal. They begin their day by getting their assigned duties listed on the screen rather than meeting with the boss over coffee. When a task is completed, it is "sent" electronically to the proper manager for checking by pushing buttons on the keyboard.

Middle layers of clerical management can be eliminated while the computer assumes monitoring and supervising functions.

But in a comprehensive electronic office, new technical job categories are created: **data clerks, operators, programmers,** and **analysts**. They work under the direction of the **manager** or **vice president of information systems,** a job which has evolved from all the old clerical information processing functions into a new, very high level position.

Companies today are competitive in part based on their ability to readily gain access to and interpret vast amounts of information and use it wisely in decision making. Thus, the manager of information systems is responsible for setting up and maintaining a data base (an electronic filing system) of all pertinent company information. It includes everything from financial information used for budgeting, forecasting, and marketing to technical information used in research and development to government reporting and employee information to interoffice communication.

The manager of information systems, usually with advanced degrees in computer science and business, is often directly responsible to the chief executive officer in the company hierarchy.

The independence offered by electronic work tools allows greater flexibility in the work place. For instance, people can work at home, using the terminal for immediate communication with co-workers.

Companies can set up duplicate satellite facilities across the country and keep in touch instantaneously.

The electronic office can be adapted to most businesses. It's being used particularly aggressively in financial and insurance industries, where daily input of data and its updating can be done much more efficiently by computer than by old ways of record-keeping.

The electronically powered information age is also fostering new businesses which sell information using high-technology tools. Shaw Data Services, with offices in New York, New Jersey, and Boston, for instance, has created a software program which it sells to financial advisers across the country. Using telecommunications and the Shaw system, the advisers an update their clients' portfolios daily with current raw data.

Shaw is using high technology to offer a service which once was a laborious clerical process. Rather than a roomful of secretaries or clerks, Shaw uses computers and **computer operators, programmers, and computer scientists.**

But despite the advances of technology in the office, many office workers, particularly a group called "9 to 5," oppose it.

They claim it marks the end of the "social office." The workers are asked to sit in separate cubicles at their individual machine terminals all day with no interaction from other humans.

They resent the "Big Brother" kind of watch over their workday which automatically tracks their productivity.

They say it also means no more career secretary, who over ten or twenty years worked her way to an indispensable position with her boss and had the earned pay and power to match that position.

Because of their dissatisfaction, the office workers have become targets for union organizing.

But it's not the technology itself which is bad, as 9 to 5 agrees. It's the way technology is implemented and how it changes our jobs and the way we work.

For instance, the secretary can end up in two very different roles as a result of office technology. She can be relegated to a support center where her job becomes simply mechanical, with no chance to participate in the work being done. Or she can evolve to a more advanced "thinking" clerical job by being asked to make decisions about the data she works with.

The increasing use of the microprocessor (a fully functioning, self-contained small computer) stimulates the potential for more people working in the latter role.

We are at a point in the evolution of the electronic office where a full range of implementations exist. Many of the more severely structured administrative support centers, for instance, have branched into more practical departmental or group pools.

The Internal Revenue Service represents one end of the spectrum of the electronic office in operation today. Of the eighty-seven thousand total IRS employees, twenty-nine thousand work at terminals in service centers. They are the information-age production workers—moving information through the pipeline using the computer as their tool.

The IRS uses a system of codes which not only allows the computer to monitor a worker's time at work on the terminal, but electronically monitors areas of activity, tasks performed, and speed and accuracy.

Richard Shriver, assistant secretary of the Treasury, is the chief adviser and policy maker concerning information technology used in the U.S. Treasury including the IRS's electronic office. He says many employers using the electronic office not only want to know when you arrive and leave work, but they want a breakdown of what you do all day.

He says that naturally breeds resentment among workers, and he sees the need for modifications.

"It must be human engineered," he says, "so that people in the information business are not repulsed by having this enormous record-keeping activity."

The electronic office operating in the IRS mode, however, is not indicative of the new-style companies which, along with technology, gain productivity and quality from employee commitment and involvement on the job.

It is certainly not the way things work at Apple Computer, which has turned its entire corporate office into a giant electronic office. Every person, from receptionist to president, has an Apple Computer sitting on his or her desk. And they all use the computer to talk to one another, gain access to company information quickly, write letters, design computers, and generally perform all the work that is done at Apple.

The computer at Apple is used as a tool for workers who by and large have acquired the new work discipline. Employers don't consider it "Big Brother."

It's easy to see there are lots of jobs Mom didn't tell you about. Here are a few more titles . . .

Human resources specialist—If you've been out looking for a job lately, you may already have realized that many companies are replacing the old personnel manager with a new human resources specialist. In fact, the whole department often has been renamed.

The name change is part of the changing work place which puts a higher value on humans as valuable resources. Instead of merely processing test scores and keeping track of Social Security numbers like the old-style personnel officer, the new-style human relations specialists do the following, according to a panel at a recent human resources symposium:
- Recruit and train.
- Create and maintain the proper corporate culture.
- Prepare employees for ongoing change.
- Plan proactive (not just reactive) compensation and benefits programs to motivate employees.

Because of the expanded duties and their effect on the overall success of the company, many new-style high-tech corporations want the human resources specialist involved in long-term strategic planning for the company. It keeps the door of communication between management and labor open.

There are schools which offer bachelor's and advanced degrees for human resources specialists. However, especially in high tech, the director of the department may be an engineer who's evolved to the company's top management team. Most departments offer entry-level positions, but many times the positions are filled from within. At one company in Research Triangle Park, a woman who went to human resources as a Kelly Girl ended up an assistant manager.

Industrial hygienist/safety manager—In a way, this job is the professional replacement for the old union shop steward whose job it was to keep an eye on safety. The industrial hygienist or safety manager works for the company, however, and the job may exist along with a union environment. The job is to monitor and evaluate the work place for occupational hazards from air contaminants and noise to chemical spills and fumes.

Prevention and training are key elements of the safety manager's duties. Each company's particular problems lend themselves to particular cures. In California at Hewlett-Packard, for instance, the industrial hygienist has developed and trained employees in procedures in the event of earthquake.

The safety manager also is the liaison between company and government for the enforcement of safety standards set by governmental agencies.

Laser technician—Laser technicians fix lasers when they break down just as robotics technicians fix robots. What's a laser? It's light with special characteristics, depending on what type of laser it is. The characteristics can be a single color or frequency of light and the laser can be made very directional. It can be focused to a very narrow beam with an intensity that burns.

The world of lasers should explode with President Reagan's commitment to further the development of laser weaponry. Today, laser optics—now we're talking mirrors with laser beams—are used in copy machines, grocery checkout scanners, and surveying tools. One of the newest applications of lasers is holograms—you know, the faces that turn and watch you as you pass by. Well, a much more practical use is being built right now by IBM in its hologram scanners. The grocery clerk can now pass the item over the scanner in any direction and the hologram will "reach up, wrap around," and find the Universal Product Code. What a timesaver that will be.

A teacher of laser optics in a reputable Florida technical institute told me even he couldn't keep up with the new applications for lasers being developed.

Laser technicians need two years' vocational school, but there aren't many schools in the country geared up to teach the full course of study yet. Nonetheless, the World Future Society predicts 2.5 million laser technicians will be working by 1990.

Quality assurance engineer—Quality is Job 1, as Ford Motor Company so aptly puts it in a national ad campaign. The new quality assurance engineer is more involved with the total end product than was the old factory inspector. And the emphasis on quality has never been greater in American industry—old-style and new-style high tech.

The quality assurance engineer inspects for precision tolerances and ingredients and also reviews contract documents to confirm completeness and accuracy. The job is so important that quality assurance staff often report directly to the corporate or division executive in charge.

Hazardous waste technician—With high technology have come chemical compounds and working environments never considered before. Thus, a growing field is opening for hazardous waste technicians who can determine the effect of various new wastes on life forms and how best to dispose of them.

Semiconductor firms which use acid solutions in the wafer "baths," for instance, are learning how to treat the waste water and recycle it. Given our poor track record at waste disposal today, it's heartening to know that an estimated half a million hazardous waste technicians will be at work by 1990.

Facilities engineer—The work environment for producing many high technology products requires very special conditions. The facilities engineer may set up a Clean Room where the air is constantly circulated to avoid tiny dust particles. He may design special air-conditioned rooms to maintain a particular temperature to house computers subject to overheating. He may design the distribution of a power system so that the demands for electrical testing don't pose a drain.

Degrees in electrical, mechanical, industrial, engineering technology, or industrial technology are good backgrounds for facilities engineers. As work place specifications become more precise, facilities engineers often need advanced degrees.

CHAPTER 7

Jobs in High Technology

"Life is different here. I think high tech is a very different kind of world. And a lot of people may feel that they're really not suited to our kind of work."

George Groneman
Sperry
Salt Lake City, Utah

The story goes that six engineering graduates from the University of Iowa shed their caps and gowns, packed into a station wagon, and headed out for Colorado right after the graduation ceremony.

They drove all night and the next day went directly to a corporate employment office on a campus-like sprawl of facilities between Denver and Boulder. Without showering or shaving, they walked in and applied for jobs.

The high-technology company hired four of them on the spot.

Not so surprising. The graduates were only proof of the mystique about the Sun Belt and the West—the jobs and the wealth that await the brave who venture out to conquer another American frontier.

The problem is many who go don't find jobs. As a matter of fact, they don't even understand the business being done there. They are put off by foreign-sounding names of companies ending with "tech" or "systems." They apply for jobs as welders when companies are hiring technicians and engineers. The engineering students, in fact, were among at least a hundred people that day who walked into the company to apply in person. They were in addition to the thousand or more applications that came in the mail that week to the same company.

Nonetheless, the engineers' story is true.

It happened that the Iowa grads had just the right electronic skills in demand at the booming computer company. In fact, the company has spent as much as a million dollars in a single year looking for such people.

This section of the book is for engineers like them who can use specific, current job information about the rapidly changing high-tech companies across the country.

But, more important, it's for the thousands who have misread the Sun Belt and Western job booms and applied for the wrong jobs. And it's for the millions more who, in the next decades, may have to shift to a high-tech growth industry from a shrinking old-style industry in order to keep working.

For all of you, this section offers simple explanations of many of the new companies, the business they do and the people they hire on an ongoing basis. The jobs identified should not be construed as want ads. Rather, they are jobs that each company says it hires for from time to time, all the time—either for turnover positions or new hire positions.

Not every company or every job in high tech in the country is included. But it does contain a good sampling of companies and jobs in the primary high-tech boom areas in the country.

It's organized by geographic location with straightforward information to clear up misconceived or preconceived notions about places like San Antonio, Texas, and Salt Lake City, Utah.

This section should not be interpreted as an invitation to pack your bags and plan your move to the Sun Belt. Some of you may well decide to do that, and I hope the information that follows will better prepare you.

For the rest of you, use the specific jobs information as you use the material that you've read thus far—to help you better understand the Jobs Revolution and our changing world of work.

The jobs information should never be used to mail resumes en masse. Rather, it should be used to select, via the comfort of your armchair, jobs that best match your skills, qualifications, and aptitudes. Once you're armed with information about what and where the jobs are, the secret to job hunting today, particularly high-tech job hunting, is in targeting, training, and tenaciousness.

Targeting. Select a job you think you'll enjoy in a geographic area where you'd like to live. Enough said about "finding yourself" in the job search. There are other books on the market that will allow you the luxury of contemplating that issue. But it boils down to selecting something you think you'd like to do and are willing to get involved in. Now, here's how to go about getting that job once you've reached your introspective, or not so introspective, decision.

The most self-defeating question I hear from people who know I'm writing a book about jobs is: "I'm a _____. Are there any jobs for _____ out there?" It's self-defeating because they ask the company or companies the same question, with little thought as to who the company is looking for.

That approach leaves a perfect out for the company, which undoubtedly has many more applications for employment than jobs available. It's easy for them to say: "No, we don't have any jobs for _____." And that's the end of it. Communication with that company is effectively shut down. And why shouldn't it be? You've gone in, remembering what you did at your last job, and that's your only point of reference—to look for a carbon copy somewhere else. In all likelihood, the company may really not have a job for _____!

The only way to job hunt today is to find out who that company needs and then try to match those needs. When you do that, your approach to the company becomes, "I'm interested in applying for one of your _____ positions." You can be confident you'll surface in the resume pile because you're talking the company's language.

You can only target a job at a company if you have information about the company and its jobs available. Let's assume you've been working as a computer programmer for two years at Company X. And you're looking for a job. You'll make headway a lot quicker in the job race if you select several companies where you'd like to work and find out what their computer programmer needs are before you send out the same generic resume to all the companies. For instance, one company may hire only entry-level programmers fresh out of school and promote the higher level positions from within. One company may call a senior programmer someone with three to five years' experience while another company may require more advanced degrees plus experience.

If you really want to work for the second company, for instance, and think you can do the job, indicate up front in a customized resume that you're applying for the job of senior programmer. Then write a cover letter and convince them why your two years' experience is worth their three-year minimum.

Job targeting means knowing about the company. Everybody says that. But nobody gets beyond Standard & Poor's and annual reports as suggested sources. What about going to the library's guide to periodicals? A public relations woman in Massachusetts told me she spent weeks in a local business library looking up current trade magazine articles about her targeted company before she ever contacted the company. When she sent a resume, her cover letter contained her suggested approach for public relations for specific projects the defense contractor was working on. That's targeting!

Again, targeting is finding out who the company is looking for, determining how you can match the position, and then asking for that position directly. And that brings us to the next key to high-tech job hunting. . . .

Training. There aren't many jobs you can even ask for in the high-tech world unless you've had some sort of training. Training is so important in the new job world that an entire section of the book was devoted to the subject. But, just in case you've missed one of the basic messages of the book thus far, or in case you immediately skipped to the jobs section, here's a final word on training.

You cannot fake it in high tech.

However, companies don't always get exactly who they're looking for (sometimes in the case of super high-end high-tech jobs, that person doesn't even exist!). So, if you think you have some of the skills and abilities the company lists as qualifications for a job, it might be worth asking to be hired along with a chance to learn the rest on the job.

Tenaciousness. The numbers tell the story. One company in Colorado has received as many as fifteen thousand applications a month while at the same time it was spending $2 million a year to recruit people. That's a lot of misguided applications that the company had to process. In the height of the recession, Alaska Airlines got so bogged down in applications—many from people not even remotely qualified—that it started charging a fee just to apply for a job, a fee it said went toward the company's processing costs.

Needless to say, it takes tenaciousness to fight those odds and come out with a job.

One of the best ways to maintain your tenaciousness in the face of some inevitable rejections is not to feel that you've lost control of the situation. And how can you possibly feel you have control when you simply go through the motions of sending out generic resumes to lots of unknown companies?

Information is the best ammunition for exercising at least some control over your job hunting. Information about the companies, the jobs, the qualifications, the rewards if you get a job, not to mention information about exactly how a particular company's application process works—it all helps alleviate the unknown which no one can fight forever. It helps you stay tenacious.

That information for a good sampling of high-tech companies and lots of jobs follows. Use it wisely, and happy hunting!

ARIZONA

Despite the Sun City image, the average age in Phoenix, Arizona, is 28.7 years—about two years below the national average.

Folks who live in Arizona retirement communities today are overshadowed by the new young professionals working in the exploding electronics industry in Phoenix and Tucson.

They populate the singles scene and posh shopping areas along the Camelback Corridor, a Phoenix crosstown street which leads east to Scottsdale, the trendy suburb oriented to youth, sunshine, and California-style boutiques.

Phoenix and Tucson offer a warm desert climate the year around, complete with saguaro cacti, oranges and grapefruits on backyard trees, and sunshine. It's hot there in the summer months—often over 100 degrees. But the dry climate makes it more bearable than the humid Midwest or Texas.

Ironically, Phoenix boasts more registered pleasure boats per capita than anywhere else in the country. They're launched into more than a half-dozen lakes within a couple hours' drive of Phoenix.

Also on the quality of life list in Phoenix are mountains (just north of the city toward Flagstaff), fishing, hunting, and skiing only two and a half hours away.

Tucson offers much the same recreational fare plus more of a Southwestern style—apparent in elegant adobe homes built in foothills overlooking the city. Many of the engineers live there, say developers.

High tech in Phoenix is not new. Motorola, Sperry, and Honeywell are the old-timers. In the last five years, they've been joined by a number of high-tech satellite operations—including Intel, GTE, and Digital Equipment Corporation.

The high-tech industry is spread in various locations around the sprawling city. One of the largest concentrations is on Interstate 17 (called Black Canyon Highway) north of Thunderbird Road.

Another is in Tempe, a southeastern suburb, home of Arizona State University (the area's academic research base) and Motorola. Tempe is also the home of many engineers—who live there in rather conventional California-style housing developments.

Phoenix welcomes the high-tech growth. Its only concern is water. For the present, however, the Central Arizona Water Project is believed to assure the area of an adequate supply to match reasonable growth.

Until a few years ago, Tucson had a no-growth attitude. People moved there and loved the foothills, mountain, and high desert beauty so much they tried to close the door behind them. As a result, while Phoenix was developing high-tech industries and jobs, Tucson was stagnant.

Then the recession hit area copper mines, and Tucson took another look at the new industries—the beautiful clean campus-like buildings, the lack of smokestacks, and the jobs. The city has attracted dozens of high-tech companies in the last few years. The most recent big prize was Garrett AiResearch which ultimately will employ 5,000—mostly engineers.

Honeywell, Large Computer Products Division (LCPD)
Phoenix

COMPANY PROFILE: This Honeywell facility designs and manufactures Honeywell's large-scale computers. There are some 5,000 employees. Professionals work in hardware, software, and systems engineering as well as all phases of manufacturing including materials control, process engineering, and factory automation.

HOW TO APPLY: Send resume to:

> Staffing Manager
> Honeywell LCPD
> P.O. Box 8000
> Phoenix, AZ 85066

HOW TO FOLLOW UP: Honeywell will contact you by phone or letter if it wants an interview. Expenses from out of state are typically paid for professional applicants. Applications are kept on file one year.

HOW TO GET THERE: You can drop off a resume in person. Take Interstate 17 north from downtown Phoenix to the Thunderbird Road exit and turn left. Honeywell is at the freeway intersection.

PROSPECTS: In mid-1983, LCPD expected active hiring only for professional/ technical positions until the general economy improved.

REWARDS: Competitive salary and benefits packages are offered in keeping with the national high-tech job market.

JOB TITLE: **Associate Engineer—Hardware/Software**

JOB DESCRIPTION: Works at entry level receiving challenging professional assignments in a variety of areas including operating systems, data base management systems, systems engineering, logic design, manufacturing engineering, and internal business systems.

QUALIFICATIONS: Bachelor's degree in electrical or industrial engineering, computer science, or math.

JOB TITLE: **Senior/Staff Engineer**

JOB DESCRIPTION: Responsible for design, development, and documentation of a specific engineering assignment or project in the areas of hardware, software, internal business systems, and/or manufacturing.

QUALIFICATIONS: Bachelor's or master's degree in relevant technical discipline plus at least five years' experience.

JOB TITLE: **Computer Test Technician**

JOB DESCRIPTION: Tests and troubleshoots a variety of computer assemblies and circuitry in order to ensure product quality and maintainability.

QUALIFICATIONS: Two-year accredited electronics technician curriculum or equivalent military experience.

JOB TITLE: **Computer Operator**

JOB DESCRIPTION: Provides hands-on operation of one or more computer systems which support research and development, manufacturing, and/or administrative operations of company.

QUALIFICATIONS: Two-year accredited computer operator curriculum or equivalent training and experience.

Sperry, Flight Systems

Phoenix

COMPANY PROFILE: This location, opened in 1957, is the headquarters for a business entity of Sperry which is a leading supplier of flight control avionics. It designs, manufactures, and markets commercial flight systems and space systems. The flight systems division in Phoenix had some 4,000 employees in mid-1983.

HOW TO APPLY: Send resume to:

Sperry
Box 21111
Phoenix, AZ 85036
Attn: Employment Department

HOW TO FOLLOW UP: You will get a letter from Sperry in three to four weeks which will indicate whether Sperry wants to interview you. If you haven't heard anything after a month, write a follow-up letter. Applications are kept on file for six months.

HOW TO GET THERE: Sperry takes walk-in applications between 8 A.M. and 4 P.M. Monday through Thursday. Most interviews are given only by appointment. From downtown Phoenix, take Interstate 17 north to the Deer Valley Road East exit. Go to the first large intersection, 19th Avenue, and turn right. You'll see Sperry on your left. Current openings are always posted in the lobby.

PROSPECTS: After a year and a half with little growth in employment, Sperry said in mid-1983 it planned an aggressive hiring mode through 1984, anticipating adding some 400 employees for both new hires and turnover. The company is primarily looking for both entry-level and experienced engineers. In mid-1983, it was not taking applications for production workers and seldom hired for administrative positions. Besides the areas listed below, Sperry is interested in engineers for CRT/display technology, mechanical engineering, radio frequency (RF) design, standards and reliability engineering, and field engineering.

REWARDS: Sperry characterizes itself as an engineering company which offers diversity and interesting work to its staff. Most research and development is systems work done in small engineering groups which can identify with finished products. The company offers the challenge of growth and the excitement of the aerospace industry. Salaries and benefits are competitive with industry standards.

JOB TITLE: **Systems Engineer**

JOB DESCRIPTION: Works with digital avionics system analysis and design, emphasizing hardware/software integration.

QUALIFICATIONS: Bachelor's degree in electrical or systems engineering with as much experience as possible with real-time systems and aircraft control law.

JOB TITLE: **Software Engineer**

JOB DESCRIPTION: Designs, develops, and implements flight software for advanced guidance and control systems (or simulators) for aircraft or space vehicles.

QUALIFICATIONS: Minimum bachelor's degree in computer science or electrical or aerospace engineering or related technical discipline plus experience with real-time programming and knowledge of Assembly and high order languages.

JOB TITLE: **Electronics Engineer**

JOB DESCRIPTION: Designs and develops microprocessor-based digital hardware or analog circuitry for use in real-time flight control and avionics systems.

QUALIFICATIONS: Bachelor's or master's degree in electrical engineering plus related experience preferred.

78

Sperry, Avionics

Phoenix

COMPANY PROFILE: In 1977 the avionics group broke off from the flight systems group of Sperry and a couple years ago moved into its own new facility in Glendale, a suburb northwest of Phoenix. The company designs and manufactures avionics for general aviation.

HOW TO APPLY: Send resume to:

Sperry
5353 W. Bell Road
Glendale, AZ 85308
Attn: Personnel Department

HOW TO FOLLOW UP: Sperry contacts applicants the company wants to interview and sends regret letters to professional applicants only. If you want to check the status of your application, you can call Personnel at (602) 863-8894. Applications are kept in an active file for six months.

HOW TO GET THERE: You can walk in to apply, but no interviews are given on the spot. Take Interstate 17 north from Phoenix to the Bell Road West exit. Go to 53rd Avenue, and you'll see Sperry on the corner.

PROSPECTS: In mid-1983, Sperry had 1,000 employees and anticipated that growing only moderately. Most needs were for engineers and technicians. No production applications were being taken.

REWARDS: Salaries and benefits are competitive with the area.

JOB TITLE: **Design Engineer—Software/Hardware**

JOB DESCRIPTION: Designs electronics and hardware for full range of avionics products. Uses computer aided design systems.

QUALIFICATIONS: Bachelor's or master's degree in electrical engineering. Hiring is for both entry-level and experienced engineers.

JOB TITLE: **Electronics Technician**

JOB DESCRIPTION: Tests products, troubleshoots equipment, and builds prototypes.

QUALIFICATIONS: Two-year associate's degree in electronics for entry level. Some experienced levels hired.

Garrett AiResearch Manufacturing Co., Electronic Systems Division

Tucson

COMPANY PROFILE: Garrett announced in late 1982 it would move one of its operations from Torrance, California, (a suburb of Los Angeles) to Tucson. Over the next few years, the military and commercial aviation contractor will set up both research and development and manufacturing facilities for designing and producing electronic systems and avionic equipment. About half the staff has a technical degree (bachelor's or above), and about a quarter are engineers.

HOW TO APPLY: Send resume or application to:

AiResearch Electronic Systems Division
Attn: Mr. Frank Washburn
7831 N. Business Park Drive
Tucson, AZ 85740

HOW TO FOLLOW UP: Garrett may not be able to respond to all applications in writing. You can write to the above address to check the status of your application. Applications are kept in an active file for one year.

HOW TO GET THERE: Garrett does take walk-in applications. From downtown Tucson, take Interstate 10 north to the Ina Road exit, proceed under the freeway to the west side access road. Turn right and follow the access road to the Peppertree Ranch sign where you turn left to Business Park Drive.

PROSPECTS: In the fall of 1983, Garrett planned to transfer about twenty people from its Torrance facility and hire another forty by year's end. The nucleus of employees was to represent a microcosm of the company—projected to have between 4,000 and 5,000 employees in the next ten years. In 1984, Garrett plans to lease a second physical building close to its planned permanent site and employ another 200 people in all categories listed below. By 1985, the company plans to be in its newly-built facilities and by the end of that year have the majority of the Electronics Systems Division of AiResearch Manufacturing Company transferred to Tucson from California.

REWARDS: Salaries are competitive with industry standards, says Garrett, and benefits include health, dental, life, and disability insurance, a stock purchase plan, and company-paid retirement.

JOB TITLE: **Design Engineer**

JOB DESCRIPTION: Performs basic design functions, including preliminary and detailed drawings, selection of materials, analysis and calculations for design criteria for whole products, parts, and components. Also coordinates design activity with engineering support groups.

QUALIFICATIONS: Bachelor's degree in an engineering discipline or equivalent plus two years' experience with knowledge of electronics, packaging, engineering mechanics, metallurgy, and/or manufacturing processes.

JOB TITLE: **Programmer**

JOB DESCRIPTION: Performs programming tasks including flow charting, logic diagrams, coding, check-out, documentation, operational installation, and program maintenance. Also develops new software programs and enhances existing ones.

QUALIFICATIONS: Bachelor's degree in computer science or equivalent plus two years' business experience as a programmer.

JOB TITLE: **Materials Analyst**

JOB DESCRIPTION: Determines requirements and scheduling for specific materials according to production demands and uses.

QUALIFICATIONS: At least three years' experience in aircraft or related industry plus familiarity with parts and materials. Some familiarity with Garrett product line.

JOB TITLE: **Electronics Technician**

JOB DESCRIPTION: Builds, repairs, and assists in troubleshooting and calibrating electronic instruments, controls, and test equipment.

QUALIFICATIONS: Working knowledge of electronic and electrical installation, math (algebra and trigonometry), and familiarity with test instruments like meters and gauges.

JOB TITLE: **Secretary**

JOB DESCRIPTION: Performs various secretarial and clerical duties, working for management level, sometimes with technical information.

QUALIFICATIONS: Some experience plus minimum 60 words per minute typing and 100 words per minute dictation.

JOB TITLE: **Assembler**

JOB DESCRIPTION: Does sub and final assembly operations on variety of precision instruments, working from blueprints and general instructions. Sometimes assembles prototype products or parts.

QUALIFICATIONS: Needs broad shop knowledge, ability to assemble and troubleshoot electro-mechanical systems, and ability to use precision equipment.

International Business Machines Corporation (IBM), General Products Division

Tucson

COMPANY PROFILE: IBM began its Tucson General Products Division operations in November 1977 and is now the metro area's second largest employer with some 5,300 people in mid-1983. General Products in Tucson develops, tests, and manufactures magnetic tape drives, mass storage systems, and high-speed laser electrophotographic system printers. The facility also manufactures direct access storage devices and assembles printed circuit cards. It's a highly automated manufacturing operation complete with robots and many employees working from computerized terminals hooked to a satellite dish collecting information from IBM facilities around the world.

HOW TO APPLY: Send resume to:

> IBM Corporation
> Employment Department
> 9000 S. Rita Road
> Tucson, AZ 85744

HOW TO FOLLOW UP: IBM responds to all applicants by mail. Applicants are asked not to telephone or visit IBM to check on their status.

HOW TO GET THERE: Walk-in applications are accepted, but interviews normally are not given at the time of application. From downtown Tucson, take Interstate 10 east about eleven miles to the Rita Road exit. You'll see IBM on your left after you exit. The employment office is in Building 040.

PROSPECTS: There are limited hiring opportunities. Most professionals are hired off college campuses.

REWARDS: Employee benefits and compensation programs are among the finest in the industry, according to IBM. The company uses a merit pay system—advancement based on performance.

JOB TITLE: **Chemical Engineer**

JOB DESCRIPTION: Entry-level engineers work in organic coating formulations and processes, plating, materials development and specifications, organic binders and substrate development, magnetic particle development, and dispersions.

QUALIFICATIONS: Bachelor's, master's, or doctorate degree in chemical engineering or equivalent knowledge/experience.

JOB TITLE: Computer Scientist

JOB DESCRIPTION: Works in logic design, digital circuit design and implementation, and maintenance of system control programs.

QUALIFICATIONS: Bachelor's, master's, or doctorate degree in computer science, mathematics, or engineering or equivalent knowledge/experience.

JOB TITLE: Electrical Engineer

JOB DESCRIPTION: Works in design and analysis of magnetic recording components, analog and digital circuit design of logic functions, microprogramming, and simulation.

QUALIFICATIONS: Bachelor's, master's, or doctorate degree in electrical engineering or equivalent knowledge/experience.

JOB TITLE: Industrial Engineer

JOB DESCRIPTION: Works with human resource planning, facilities planning, plant layout, workload forecasting, and manufacturing capacity planning.

QUALIFICATIONS: Bachelor's or master's degree in industrial engineering or equivalent knowledge/experience.

JOB TITLE: Materials/Metallurgy/Ceramic Engineer

JOB DESCRIPTION: Works with ceramic materials, polymers, and metallurgical systems in connection with materials and process development and failure analysis.

QUALIFICATIONS: Bachelor's, master's, or doctorate degree in materials, metallurgy, or ceramic engineering or equivalent knowledge/experience.

JOB TITLE: Mechanical Engineer

JOB DESCRIPTION: Involved in development of product systems for flexible magnetic media mechanical processes, tool development, tribology and wear, fluid dynamics, and servo-mechanisms.

QUALIFICATIONS: Bachelor's, master's, or doctorate degree in mechanical engineering or equivalent knowledge/experience.

JOB TITLE: Electronics Technician

JOB DESCRIPTION: Performs test, defect analysis, and repair on electrical/electro-mechanical units and is skilled in use of specialized test equipment such as oscilloscopes, meters, etc.

QUALIFICATIONS: Two-year associate's degree in electronics or equivalent knowledge/experience.

JOB TITLE: **Assembler**

JOB DESCRIPTION: Assembles complete functional units or complex subassemblies. Uses basic and specialized tools and gauges.

QUALIFICATIONS: Various levels of appropriate education and/or experience.

Hamilton Test Systems

Tucson

COMPANY PROFILE: Hamilton Test, a unit of United Technologies, is one of the world's leading manufacturers of electronic control and testing equipment. The company's products are used to run elevators, regulate air conditioning systems, and test automobile engines. Hamilton also makes vehicle emission testing equipment and operates an emission testing program for the state of Arizona and several other cities and states across the country. Tucson is the company's headquarters.

HOW TO APPLY: Send resume to:

Hamilton Test Systems
2301 N. Forbes Blvd.
Tucson, AZ 85745
Attn: Personnel

HOW TO FOLLOW UP: Hamilton does respond by mail to all applications for professional positions. Others are contacted only if there's an immediate interest in the applicant. All applications are kept on file for one year. You can call the general number, (602) 792-3260, for information on the status of your application.

HOW TO GET THERE: You can fill out an application or drop off a resume in person in the main lobby, but the company cannot give interviews on the spot. From downtown Tucson, take Interstate 10 west to the Grant exit. Turn left (west) and go a couple of blocks to Forbes and turn left. Hamilton Test Systems is in the Broadbent Interstate Center. It's the first building on your right.

PROSPECTS: In mid-1983, Hamilton had about 425 employees in Tucson and anticipated moderate growth, particularly in engineering positions. The company says it has more than enough applications on file from local residents for semi-skilled positions, like assembler.

REWARDS: Hamilton says its salaries and benefits are competitive, and it offers relocation packages for professionals.

JOB TITLE: **Design Engineer—Hardware/Software**

JOB DESCRIPTION: Designs microprocessor systems and develops software engineering systems.

QUALIFICATIONS: There are a full range of positions from entry level requiring only a bachelor's degree in electrical engineering or computer science to advanced positions requiring advanced degrees and up to ten years' experience.

JOB TITLE: **Drafter**

JOB DESCRIPTION: Makes finished drawings which range from detailing simple to complex parts to the design and layout of printed circuit boards.

QUALIFICATIONS: There are a range of positions from entry level requiring only a two-year drafting degree or equivalent experience to up to ten years' experience.

JOB TITLE: **Electronics Technician**

JOB DESCRIPTION: Tests, troubleshoots, and repairs analog and digital circuitry of production units.

QUALIFICATIONS: Two-year associate's degree in electronics or equivalent experience.

Kitt Peak National Observatory

Tucson

COMPANY PROFILE: Kitt Peak, established in 1958, is the ground-based national optical astronomy center in the United States. It is funded by the National Science Foundation and operated by a nonprofit corporation, the Association of Universities for Research in Astronomy (AURA, Inc.). The observatory was set up on Kitt Peak, some fifty-five miles west of Tucson, to offer a high and clear vantage point to the nation's astronomers and universities, many situated in dense urban areas at low elevations. Today, Kitt Peak operates both at the observatory and at a site in Tucson. It has built some sixty-five optical instruments and fourteen telescopes. Staff members are involved in basic research and support services for scientists across the country.

HOW TO APPLY: Send resume to:

> Personnel Manager
> Kitt Peak National Observatory
> P.O. Box 26732
> Tucson, AZ 85726

HOW TO FOLLOW UP: Kitt Peak does respond to all resumes, but it may take as long as a couple of months. The observatory generally interviews three or four top candidates for each position to be filled.

HOW TO GET THERE: You can drop off a resume in person. From the Tucson Airport, take Valencia Road east about two miles to Palo Verde Boulevard and turn left or north. Go about seven miles to Speedway Boulevard, and turn left or west. Go two miles to Cherry Boulevard, turn left or south, go two blocks, and you'll see Kitt Peak's Tucson headquarters on the southeast corner. The address is 950 North Cherry Boulevard.

PROSPECTS: In mid-1983, Kitt Peak had some 270 permanent employees and was planning to hire a small number of new people, particularly highly skilled and experienced astronomers and engineers. The observatory is currently involved in the design work for the fifteen-meter National New Technology Telescope (NNTT). The observatory will select one of two concepts for the telescope in the spring of 1984 and then begin final design work. In mid-1983, Kitt Peak was looking for active optics and instrumentation engineers for the NNTT project. In addition, people are hired in small numbers on an ongoing basis for the positions listed below.

REWARDS: Although actual salaries for professionals are not always as high as industry pays, Kitt Peak says the work environment and special benefits make the total job package very competitive. Among benefits are five weeks annual vacation, an excellent retirement package, and a work environment of basic research free of the politics of selling new contracts and customer modifications. Engineers have state-of-the-art equipment and private offices, each with a terminal hooked into five computers.

JOB TITLE: **Scientists—Astronomers, Physicists**

JOB DESCRIPTION: Research scientists spend up to 50 percent of their time doing pure, independent research. The balance is spent working on projects associated with universities and other scientists across the country. Support scientists spend about 10 percent of their time doing research and the balance doing support work with visiting scientists.

QUALIFICATIONS: Minimum doctorate degree in astronomy or physics.

JOB TITLE: **Engineers—Electronics/Mechanical/Structural/Engineering Physicists/Optical**

JOB DESCRIPTION   Design, develop, implement, and maintain special equipment (telescopes and instrumentation) for ground-based astronomers.

QUALIFICATIONS: Bachelor's or master's degree in appropriate engineering discipline plus some positions require from five to seven years' experience.

JOB TITLE: **Programmer**

JOB DESCRIPTION: Writes real-time software applications in FORTH for data acquisition and telescope operations, software in FORTRAN and C for reduction and analysis of astronomical data, and/or special operating systems.

QUALIFICATIONS: Minimum bachelor's degree in computer science, astronomy, physics, or engineering and three years' experience. Full range of positions up to doctorate level.

JOB TITLE: **Large Telescope Operator (LTO)**

JOB DESCRIPTION: Actually operates the telescopes and major astronomical instruments to track particular stars and/or gather data. Works at the mountain facility for six days and nights, then gets three days off.

QUALIFICATIONS: Bachelor's degree in astronomy or physics. Entry-level position with no experience required.

CALIFORNIA

In 1950, the lush rolling California valley between Palo Alto to the north and San Jose to the south was known mostly for its prune and pear orchards. There were three high-tech firms—though no one called them that then.

Today at least 2,000 high-tech firms, wall-to-wall people, jammed freeways, and outrageously priced land and homes have replaced the fruit trees in the well-recognized home of high tech—Silicon Valley.

Many new, highly successful companies have been started there in someone's garage or spare bedroom—often with nothing more than an idea. A fair number have turned into million and billion dollar enterprises in remarkably short times. Those successes continue to breed the new entrepreneurs who apply brilliant minds with high hopes and endless energy to the development of new technologies and products.

Although there are tens of thousands of high-tech manufacturing jobs in Silicon Valley, there are at least as many jobs for engineers and scientists in research areas. Many companies that have expanded beyond California to the high-tech boom towns across the Sun Belt maintain major research and development facilities near their Silicon Valley corporate offices.

Stanford University in Palo Alto, one of two top-rated sources of engineering graduates for high-tech companies, supplies the talent and the central research base for the area.

Venture capital for start-up companies is bountiful.

The climate is predominently sunny California. San Francisco, just an hour north, offers night life and cultural events. Many of the larger companies have integrated the California outdoor life-style into company campuses with full fledged athletic facilities for employees.

A second major high-tech growth area developing in Southern California is San Diego. Community spokesmen say they get people and companies who don't want to live in the rat race of Silicon Valley, but don't want to leave California.

San Diego offers a diverse geography—ranging from beach front, desert, mountain, to ranchland—all within driving distance to its growing high-tech development areas.

The city is attracting many Japanese companies, like Kyocera International, in part because it's the closest American port to the Pacific Basin.

The high-tech industrial area around Balboa Road, north of downtown San Diego, is like a mini-Silicon Valley—company after company along surburban-style streets. About thirty miles north of San Diego is Rancho

Bernardo, the site of major high-tech facilities like Sony and Hewlett-Packard and a booming development of housing and shops.

Between Balboa Road and Rancho Bernardo is an area called the Golden Triangle which has some high-tech business and is shopping for more.

San Diego needs jobs to help put displaced tuna fishermen and ship-builders back to work. Area development spokemen said in mid-1983 some 35,000 people were employed in electronics in San Diego. They hope to double that number by 1990.

Advanced Micro Devices, Inc. (AMD)

Silicon Valley; Sunnyvale

COMPANY PROFILE: For the last seven years, Advanced Micro Devices has been the fastest growing major publicly held U.S. integrated circuit maker. The company, with more than 11,000 employees in mid-1983, was founded in 1969 by Jerry Sanders, former worldwide marketing director for Fairchild Semiconductor. The aim was to offer a variety of more and more advanced integrated circuits with an emphasis on quality. Today AMD serves professional markets in communication, instrumentation, and computation with more than 500 different integrated circuits (ICs)—nearly half of which are proprietary. The ICs, developed with both bipolar and MOS (metal oxide silicon) technologies, are used in microprocessor, peripheral, memory, analog, and logic product applications. The Sunnyvale facility houses research and development, corporate administration, and manufacturing operations which together employ about 4,500 people. Satellite facilities are in Austin and San Antonio, Texas.

HOW TO APPLY: Send resume or application to:

Advanced Micro Devices (MS 57)
901 Thompson Place
Box 3453
Sunnyvale, CA 94088

HOW TO FOLLOW UP: AMD will send you an acknowledgment letter with an indication of the company's immediate interest in you within two to three weeks. If you want to call for your status after that time, call the main number, (408) 732-2400, and ask for Employment. Applications are kept on file for one year.

HOW TO GET THERE: AMD accepts walk-in applications, but does not give unscheduled interviews. Heading south from San Francisco on Highway 101, take the Lawrence Expressway south, or right, to the second stoplight, Arques Avenue. Turn right to the second stoplight again, which is DeGuigne, and turn right. The first street on your left is Thompson Place. Continue a half block to Stewart Drive, and turn right. AMD's personnel office is at 898 Stewart.

PROSPECTS: AMD has grown an average 30 percent each year and anticipates that continuing or bettering through 1984. The company is in an especially accelerated growth mode in its college hiring. AMD recruits at forty-six colleges nationally and planned on some 200 new hires in the 1982-1983 school year. The major professional job titles are listed below. College graduates are hired for entry-level positions, and AMD says it also looks for experienced people in the same categories.

REWARDS: AMD has a formal no layoff policy in addition to competitive salaries and benefits. Although the company doesn't have formal flex hours, it does offer flexible working conditions for professionals.

Job Title: **Applications Engineer**

Job Description: Works with customers on technical level to develop understanding of their semiconductor needs and future requirements. Translates those needs into feasible block diagrams and specifications for design engineers. May conceive new products custom designed for customer needs.

Qualifications: Bachelor's or master's degree in electrical engineering, computer science, or computer engineering.

Job Title: **Design Engineer**

Job Description: Designs, analyzes, and characterizes complex, state-of-the-art analog, digital, and linear integrated circuits, including LSI (large scale integration) and VLSI (very large scale integration) memories, microprocessors, and peripherals. Uses advanced MOS (metal oxide silicon) and bipolar technology, TTL, Schottky TTL, and ECL.

Qualifications: Bachelor's, master's, or Ph.D. in electrical or computer engineering, or solid state physics, or computer aided design (CAD).

Job Title: **Product Engineer**

Job Description: Evaluates wafer products in order to increase yield enhancement while maintaining and improving product reliability and production flow.

Qualifications: Bachelor's or master's degree in electrical engineering, computer engineering, or solid state physics.

Job Title: **Process Sustaining/Process Development Engineer**

Job Description: Develops advanced processes for the development and production of state-of-the-art integrated circuits using advanced CMOS, NMOS, and bipolar process technologies, including photolithography technology, diffusion, multi-layer metalization, ion implantation, plasma etching, and deposition techniques.

Qualifications: Bachelor's, master's, or Ph.D. in electrical or chemical engineering, solid state physics, materials science.

Job Title: **Test Engineer**

Job Description: Selects production testing equipment and develops hardware and software for production testing and test operating systems.

Qualifications: Bachelor's or master's degree in electrical or computer engineering or computer science.

JOB TITLE: **Product Marketing Engineer**

JOB DESCRIPTION: Participates in pricing strategies, forecasting, contract negotiation, strategic planning, market assessment, and merchandising.

QUALIFICATIONS: Bachelor's or master's in electrical engineering, master's in business administration preferred.

JOB TITLE: **Corporate Planning Analyst**

JOB DESCRIPTION: Develops and maintains annual business plan, forecasts, budgets, and cash flows. Analyzes industry and market trends.

QUALIFICATIONS: Master's in business administration.

JOB TITLE: **Product Line Analyst**

JOB DESCRIPTION: Analyzes all phases of the group's products and monitors product line performance for top management.

QUALIFICATIONS: Master's in business administration.

JOB TITLE: **Information Systems Programmer**

JOB DESCRIPTION: Writes, maintains, and analyzes computer programs for internal business uses. Tests and debugs programs, prepares documentation, and determines techniques used in writing programs.

QUALIFICATIONS: Bachelor's degree in business, math, statistics, or computer science.

JOB TITLE: **Sales Engineer**

JOB DESCRIPTION: Provides the critical interface between customer, field sales force, and company operating groups. Develops approaches to account penetration and sales growth.

QUALIFICATIONS: Bachelor's or master's degree in electrical engineering or computer engineering.

JOB TITLE: **CAD/Design Automation Engineer**

JOB DESCRIPTION: Develops, evaluates, and installs software to assist in the design of VLSI circuits. Works closely with a variety of CAD system users to develop effective man-machine interfaces.

QUALIFICATIONS: Master's or Ph.D. in electrical engineering or computer science.

Apple Computer, Inc.

Silicon Valley; Cupertino

COMPANY PROFILE: Apple Computer is one of the most successful and fastest growing personal computer manufacturers in the world. It was started in California fairy tale fashion in 1975 by Steven Jobs, the marketing whiz, and Stephen Wozniak, the computer whiz. Today, the team at Apple believes it is on a "mission" to make personal computers as common as your telephone or television. In the California headquarters, Apple designs, develops, produces, markets, and services microprocessor-based personal computers and related software and peripheral products. The only other American manufacturing site is in Carrollton, Texas (see Dallas section). Apple also manufactures its products in Ireland.

HOW TO APPLY: Send resumes to:

> Apple Computer, Inc.
> 20525 Mariani Ave.
> Cupertino, CA 95014
> Attn: Staffing

HOW TO FOLLOW UP: Apple replies by letter to every resume in about two weeks. You can call a main phone number, (408) 996-1010, to be sure your resume was received, but Apple can't give much information by phone.

HOW TO GET THERE: Walk-in applications and resumes are welcome and can be dropped off with a receptionist during business hours at Apple's human resources office, at 10495 Bandley Drive in Cupertino. However, you'll only get an interview by appointment after the resume is reviewed. The human resources office is in Cupertino in Santa Clara County, California. It's approximately two blocks south of the intersection of Highway 280 and De Anza Boulevard (also called Saratoga-Sunnyvale or Highway 9). Turn west off De Anza on Mariani Avenue and proceed one block to Bandley Drive.

PROSPECTS: Apple had 4,100 employees in mid-1983 and anticipated growing to 4,800 by 1984. The company has had explosive growth in its short history and anticipates that continuing. Apple says it has high satisfaction from people on the job, thus low turnover. So, openings are generally for new hires. Apple says it's looking for "bright, talented people." Since Chairman of the Board Steven Jobs didn't even get a college degree, the company looks at applicants individually—weighing experience and proven talent as heavily as academics.

REWARDS: Apple claims it is committed to being among the top companies in the computer industry in providing a total compensation and benefits package. One unusual perk for all employees at Apple is a "Loan to Own" program in which every employee has access to an Apple computer which they can take home for their personal use. After a year on the job, the computer is theirs to keep. Salaries are determined according to very individualistic reviews of a person's experience, academics, and abilities.

JOB TITLE: **Human Resources Specialist**

JOB DESCRIPTION: Directs activity in staffing, compensation, training, college recruiting, or benefits.

QUALIFICATIONS: Bachelor's degree in business administration plus up to four years' experience, depending on position.

JOB TITLE: **Financial Analyst**

JOB DESCRIPTION: Provides technical financial support to planning and forecasting process.

QUALIFICATIONS: Bachelor's degree in finance or accounting plus three years' experience or the equivalent.

JOB TITLE: **Cost Accountant**

JOB DESCRIPTION: Collects, summarizes, and records cost and inventory data. This is the entry-level professional accounting position.

QUALIFICATIONS: Bachelor's degree in accounting or three years' experience.

JOB TITLE: **Programmer Analyst**

JOB DESCRIPTION: Designs and writes detailed program designs for business applications needed internally at Apple. This is an entry-level technical position for the computer program analysis function.

QUALIFICATIONS: Bachelor's degree in scientific or business-related field plus one and a half years' programming experience or three years' programming experience.

JOB TITLE: **Programmer C**

JOB DESCRIPTION: Helps write programs for internal Apple business applications. Codes and tests business applications, documents newly written or modified programs. This also is an entry-level technical position for computer programming.

QUALIFICATIONS: Bachelor's degree in scientific or business-related field or six months of programming experience.

JOB TITLE: **Customer Support Program Specialist**

JOB DESCRIPTION: Coordinates customer support programs and establishes administrative policies in the support centers. Helps in introduction and implementation of new products and programs.

QUALIFICATIONS: Bachelor's degree plus three to five years' experience in implementing procedures. Very strong communications skills necessary.

JOB TITLE: **Customer Support Specialist**

JOB DESCRIPTION: Interfaces on day-to-day basis with customer base, dealer network, sales, and credit to provide support for selected accounts or enhance further sales.

QUALIFICATIONS: Bachelor's degree plus two years' experience or the equivalent experience in public/customer support and satisfaction.

JOB TITLE: **Customer Relations Specialist**

JOB DESCRIPTION: Handles customer inquiries by telephone or written correspondence. Occasional travel required.

QUALIFICATIONS: Associates' degree with four years' experience or bachelor's degree with one year's experience or equivalent experience in communications, public relations, customer relations, and/or sales.

JOB TITLE: **Service/Support Engineer**

JOB DESCRIPTION: Provides technical support of Apple's level one service center network and/or regional service centers.

QUALIFICATIONS: Bachelor's degree in scientific discipline plus up to four years' experience or equivalent experience with computer service/support. Must have good verbal and written communications skills as well.

JOB TITLE: **Service/Support Training Specialist**

JOB DESCRIPTION: Conducts various post-sale oriented courses in personal computer applications, technical or service areas.

QUALIFICATIONS: Bachelor's degree plus four years' experience or equivalent experience. Microcomputer experience preferred.

JOB TITLE: **Public Relations Specialist**

JOB DESCRIPTION: Assists in developing long range public relations strategies in corporate or product areas and ensures timely and effective press relations.

QUALIFICATIONS: Bachelor's degree in English, journalism, or business plus three years in news publications, public relations agency, corporate public relations in a consumer products environment, or equivalent experience.

JOB TITLE: **Market Research Analyst**

JOB DESCRIPTION: Provides support for product planning through research and analysis of Apple's markets, competitive product mix, and specified product markets.

QUALIFICATIONS: Bachelor's degree plus up to four years' experience in marketing/marketing research.

JOB TITLE: **Creative Services Coordinator**

JOB DESCRIPTION: Coordinates all creative service projects, assures that production is timely, cost effective, and meets quality standards.

QUALIFICATIONS: Associate's degree in graphics/marketing plus two to six years' experience in graphic, print, and photography production or advertising or market communications.

JOB TITLE: **Graphics Designer**

JOB DESCRIPTION: Designs promotional, point-of-sale, informational material within the parameters of the "Apple Look."

QUALIFICATIONS: Associate's degree plus two to six years' design experience. Need an acceptable portfolio and knowledge of print process and mechanical art production.

JOB TITLE: **Sales Promotion Planner**

JOB DESCRIPTION: Develops strategies and concepts and then implements product promotions to support the sales effort.

QUALIFICATIONS: Bachelor's degree plus four years of sales promotion experience or equivalent experience.

JOB TITLE: **Marketing Support Representative**

JOB DESCRIPTION: Identifies and prevents sales or service problems as Apple representative at the customer site. Provides account executive support, product familiarization, and helps solve maintenance problems.

QUALIFICATIONS: Bachelor's degree plus one or two years in sales or sales support or equivalent experience.

JOB TITLE: **Sales Training and Development Specialist**

JOB DESCRIPTION: Designs and implements sales training programs as they relate to internal, field, rep, and dealer sales personnel.

QUALIFICATIONS: Bachelor's degree in a training related field plus one to five years' experience.

JOB TITLE: **Engineer—Software**

JOB DESCRIPTION: Works on the design team to specifically design the software operating systems of new products, using the programming languages of Assembly and Pascal.

QUALIFICATIONS: Master's degree in computer science or equivalent plus significant experience (at least two years) in low level systems software.

JOB TITLE: **Engineer—Hardware**

JOB DESCRIPTION: Works on design team to design the electronic hardware that runs the basic logic of the computer.

QUALIFICATIONS: Master's degree in electrical engineering or equivalent plus significant experience (two years minimum) in digital, analog, or very large scale integration specialties.

JOB TITLE: **Engineer—Product Design**

JOB DESCRIPTION: Works on the design team to design the physical, mechanical facets of the computer.

QUALIFICATIONS: Master's degree in industrial design or tooling design or equivalent experience plus at least two years' experience.

JOB TITLE: **Mechanical Technician**

JOB DESCRIPTION: Works on design team as aide to product design engineers.

QUALIFICATIONS: Two-year associate's degree in mechanical technician course plus at least two years' experience.

JOB TITLE: **Electronics Technician**

JOB DESCRIPTION: Works on design team as aide to software and hardware engineers.

QUALIFICATIONS: Two-year associate's degree in electronics technician course plus at least two years' experience.

JOB TITLE: **Electro-Mechanical Drafter**

JOB DESCRIPTION: Works on design team as an aide to engineers to draft mechanical and physical designs for new products.

QUALIFICATIONS: Two-year associate's degree in drafting plus at least two years' experience in computer aided design system.

JOB TITLE: **Computer Aided Design Technician**

JOB DESCRIPTION: Takes engineers' and drafters' roughs for circuit designs and converts them into working documents by digitizing with computer aided design (CAD).

QUALIFICATIONS: Two-year associate's degree in CAD plus at least two years' experience.

JOB TIP: Because of the flexible, yet immediate, needs for people in various stages of designing new computer products, Apple uses a number of temporary employees. They are hired for short periods of intense work in various specialties, as well as low skill areas.

The most common temporary job titles are: materials processor (that's a shipping clerk), assembler (to help put together prototypes), electronics technician (mostly for testing prototypes), area associates (clerks and secretaries, electronic office style), and receptionists. If you want to give temporary employment a try, these are the agencies that Apple contracts with in the Silicon Valley area: Manpower, Adia, Kelly, Jobs Unlimited, Personalized, and Remedy.

Data General Corporation

Silicon Valley; Sunnyvale

COMPANY PROFILE: This facility of Data General Corporation, headquartered in Westboro, Massachusetts, designs and produces semiconductors for use in Data General products. It was opened in 1972 and in mid-1983 had just under 400 employees.

HOW TO APPLY: Send resume to:

Data General
433 N. Mathilda Ave.
Sunnyvale, CA 94086

HOW TO FOLLOW UP: You will get an acknowledgment of your resume and a letter indicating Data General's interest in you following that. You can call a main number, (408) 739-9200, extension 5502, to learn the status of your resume.

HOW TO GET THERE: You can walk in to apply. Coming from San Francisco, take Highway 101 south to the Mathilda Avenue exit. Turn south (right) on Mathilda. Data General is just past the third light on your right.

PROSPECTS: This facililty anticipates moderate growth in 1984, roughly an increase of 10 percent.

REWARDS: Same as Data General employees corporate-wide. See the Data General listing for Boston, page 164.

JOB TITLE: **Wafer Fab Operator**

JOB DESCRIPTION: Works in the front end area, performing various precision tasks in the production of semiconductors.

QUALIFICATIONS: Need some wafer fabrication experience.

JOB TITLE: **Process/Sustaining Engineer**

JOB DESCRIPTION: Works in the fab area to continuously improve the wafer fab process.

QUALIFICATIONS: Bachelor's degree in chemical engineering, physics, or materials science. Full range of jobs from entry level to jobs requiring experience.

JOB TITLE: **Process Engineer**

JOB DESCRIPTION: Designs and develops processes for manufacturing semiconductors.

QUALIFICATIONS: Same as process/sustaining engineer.

JOB TITLE: **Product Engineer**

JOB DESCRIPTION: Interfaces with design and manufacturing groups to develop manufacturing and testing procedures.

QUALIFICATIONS: Bachelor's degree in electrical engineering and all levels of experience.

JOB TITLE: **Design Engineer**

JOB DESCRIPTION: Designs the chip electronics using bipolar and MOS (metal oxide silicon) technologies.

QUALIFICATIONS: Bachelor's degree in electrical engineering and all levels of experience.

Hewlett-Packard

Silicon Valley; Palo Alto

COMPANY PROFILE: Hewlett-Packard, one of Silicon Valley's original high-tech companies, was started as a one-product company in 1939 in Dave Packard's garage. The two men developed technology that changed the course of oscillator design for years to come. Today the company operates manufacturing facilities in nine states and seven countries. It produces some 4,500 products and employs some 67,000 people. About 17,000 work in Silicon Valley at a host of divisions spread from one end of the valley to the other. In general terms, HP designs, manufactures, and markets the following products: computers, computer-based systems and peripherals; calculators and personal computing products; electronic test and measuring instruments and systems; medical electronic products; analytical instrumentation; solid-state components.

In addition to divisions which produce those products, HP has extensive research and development (R&D) facilities and sales and service staffs. In Silicon Valley, the company designs and manufactures product lines as indicated below and maintains its corporate offices.

For a variety of reasons, including increased automation in its manufacturing facilities and changing technologies, HP anticipates hiring fewer hourly production workers and more professional workers in all its divisions across the country. While there are a myriad of job titles representing nearly every current technology, the ones listed below are the major categories in which HP hires on an ongoing basis.

HOW TO APPLY: If you're applying for a professional position, you can apply to a central address where your resume will be entered into a central data base.

Send resume to:

> Corporate Staffing, 20AD
> Hewlett-Packard
> 3000 Hanover St.
> Palo Alto, CA 94304

If you're applying for an hourly job, you can apply directly to the division as listed below:

> Application Marketing Division
> 19320 Pruneridge Ave.
> Cupertino, CA 95014

> Computer Supplies Operation A5
> 1320 Kifer Road
> Sunnyvale, CA 94086

Computer Support Division
19310 Pruneridge Ave.
Cupertino, CA 95014

Computer Systems Division
19447 Pruneridge Ave.
Cupertino, CA 95014

Corporate Parts Center
333 Logue Ave.
P.O. Box 7022
Mountain View, CA 94043

Cupertino Integrated Circuits
10900 Wolfe Road
Cupertino, CA 95014

Data Systems Division
11000 Wolfe Road
Cupertino, CA 95014

HP Labs
1501 Page Mill Road
Palo Alto, CA 94304

Information Networks Division
19420 Homestead Road
Cupertino, CA 95014

Instrument Support Division
690 E. Middlefield Road
Mountain View, CA 94042

Interface Products Operation
640 Page Mill Road
Palo Alto, CA 94304

Manufacturing Productivity Division
370 W. Trimble Road
San Jose, CA 95131

Microwave Semiconductor Division
350 W. Trimble Road
San Jose, CA 95131

Optoelectronics Division
640 Page Mill Road
Palo Alto, CA 94304

Personal Office Computer
974 East Arques
Sunnyvale, CA 94086

Santa Clara Division
5301 Stevens Creek Blvd.
Santa Clara, CA 95050

Scientific Instruments Division
1601 California Ave.
Palo Alto, CA 94304

Stanford Park Division
1501 Page Mill Road
Palo Alto, CA 94304

Systems Re-Marketing
1324 Kifer Road
Sunnyvale, CA 94086

How to Follow Up: HP does acknowledge all applications and resumes. They are then reviewed by the proper division and/or manager to determine whether to call you for an interview. Resumes are kept active for six months, and HP requests that you not send more than one during that time.

How to Get There: You can apply in person at any HP division. If you don't know the area, you can pick up a map that shows HP locations throughout Silicon Valley from the main headquarters at 3000 Hanover. To get there, take Highway 101 south from San Franciso to the Oregon exit in Palo Alto. Turn west and follow until the street becomes Page Mill Road. Hanover is just past El Camino Real. You'll see Hewlett-Packard on your left. Or you can call a main number, (415) 857-1501, for more information.

Prospects: HP does most recruiting for professionals on college campuses. The company philosophy calls for hiring young talent and molding it in the HP way. In 1983, HP nationally planned to hire 1,000 college graduates mostly for positions listed below. The steady growth mode was anticipated to continue through calendar 1984.

Rewards: Since its beginning, based on a philosophy of respect and concern for employees as individuals, Hewlett-Packard has won praise from outsiders and its employees alike as being one of America's best companies to work for. The company has a long history of no layoffs. Flex hours are the rule company-wide. Management is by objective and "walking around"—an extension of the open door employer-employee communication policy. Communciation, informality, and respect for people all result in HP maintaining a reputation for turning out exceptional quality products.

Job Title: **Development Engineer—Hardware/Software**

Job Description: As part of research and development design team, works with team and individually to develop new products. Areas of study include solid-state materials and processes, software studies, device physics and design, quantum electronics, lasers and optics, magnetics, computer architecture, metallic and dialectric thin films, analog and digital circuitry, resonance physics, fluid mechanics, advanced molding technology, piezoelectricity, and electronic instruments and instrumentation systems.

QUALIFICATIONS: Bachelor's degree in electrical engineering, computer science, or related discipline.

JOB TITLE: **Production Engineer**

JOB DESCRIPTION: As a member of the manufacturing team, works to solve problems and improve the efficiency of the manufacture of an assigned product line. Brings new products from R&D to manufacturing stage, develops and implements testing and assembly methods, and conducts product cost studies to improve profitability while maintaining and/or improving product quality.

QUALIFICATIONS: Bachelor's degree in electrical, mechanical, or industrial engineering. Master's degree in engineering or business administration preferred.

JOB TITLE: **Fabrication (Manufacturing) Engineer**

JOB DESCRIPTION: Works with both R&D and manufacturing teams to ensure smooth transition of new products from one to the other. Duties include determining manufacturing processes for fabricated parts, deciding whether to produce in-house or buy from outside vendor, determining best techniques and tools for making highest quality products at lowest cost.

QUALIFICATIONS: Bachelor's degree in mechanical or industrial engineering or related discipline. Master's degree in engineering or business administration preferred.

JOB TITLE: **Manufacturing Process Engineer**

JOB DESCRIPTION: Monitors, evaluates, and improves processes for fabrication of state-of-the-art integrated circuits.

QUALIFICATIONS: Bachelor's degree in engineering or physical sciences. Master's degree preferred.

JOB TITLE: **Materials Engineer**

JOB DESCRIPTION: Recommends best parts and vendors and sets up technical parts testing and procurement procedures to meet and improve product requirements.

QUALIFICATIONS: Bachelor's degree in electrical or mechanical engineering. Master's degree in engineering or business administration preferred.

JOB TITLE: **Buyer, Scheduler**

JOB DESCRIPTION: Buyer procures materials, components, and services and manages inventories. Scheduler makes sure technical components are in right place at right time in manufacturing process. Either job can lead to project manager role.

QUALIFICATIONS: Bachelor's degree in business, master's in business administration preferred.

JOB TITLE: **Product Assurance Engineer**

JOB DESCRIPTION: Works in both research and development and manufacturing stages to assure product reliability in areas of thermal and software reliability. Designs and develops automated test systems for those properties.

QUALIFICATIONS: Bachelor's degree in electrical, mechanical, or industrial engineering. Master's degree in engineering or business administration preferred.

JOB TITLE: **Facilities Engineer**

JOB DESCRIPTION: Member of facilities team which is responsible for modification of buildings, building equipment, and utilities maintenance. Special assignments could include installation of air conditioning systems for computer rooms, metal painting, and fabrication and integrated circuit processes; provision of electrical power distribution systems for wiring, assembly, and test operations; and layout, construction, and start-up of clean rooms.

QUALIFICATIONS: Bachelor's degree in electrical, mechanical, or industrial engineering, engineering technology, or industrial technology. Master's degree in electrical, mechanical, or industrial engineering preferred.

JOB TITLE: **Marketing Engineer**

JOB DESCRIPTION: May be assigned to one of the following areas:

Product Marketing—Uses market analysis to contribute to product definition, establishes market plan for product, plans and coordinates promotional and sales efforts, develops sales training programs, including technical literature.

Sales Development and Support—Creates regionally-tailored sales plans, sets sales quotas, and prepares sales forecasts.

Applications Engineering—Helps develop sales measurement techniques in existing and new market areas.

Product Support—Trains and backs up customer representatives and customers in maintenance of HP equipment.

QUALIFICATIONS: Bachelor's degree in engineering or related scientific discipline. Master's degree preferred.

JOB TITLE: **Field Sales Representative**

JOB DESCRIPTION: Sells HP products directly to customer using a consultative approach, i.e., comprehensively studying and satisfying customer needs with just the right combination of HP products.

QUALIFICATIONS: Bachelor's degree in engineering, physics, mathematics, chemistry, computer science, the life sciences or, related disciplines. Starting as a staff sales representative, you spend eight to ten months in formal classroom training and on-the-job experience learning HP products and client applications.

JOB TITLE: **Systems Representative**

JOB DESCRIPTION: Backs up field sales staff with technical support for applying HP equipment to meet customer needs, demonstrating products to customers, and recommending and implementing training programs for customer staffs.

QUALIFICATIONS: Bachelor's degree in engineering, physics, mathematics, computer science, life sciences, medical electronics, or related discipline. Job begins with twelve to eighteen months classroom training in commercial computer systems, instrumentation systems, logic measurements, medical systems, or systems for analytical chemistry, followed by three to nine months of field training.

JOB TITLE: **Customer Representative**

JOB DESCRIPTION: Responsible for on-site installation of major HP systems and equipment and ongoing preventative maintenance, repair, and calibration after installation.

QUALIFICATIONS: Bachelor's degree in electronic engineering, electronic engineering technology, physics, mathematics, biomedical engineering, or related discipline. Five to seven months of on-the-job training required before being assigned to accounts.

JOB TITLE: **Programmer, Analyst**

JOB DESCRIPTION: At entry level, performs moderately complex computer programming functions, including system documentation, and development of test data and routines. Can evolve to project leader responsible for directing system development and implementation.

QUALIFICATIONS: Bachelor's degree in computer science or related discipline. Master's degree in computer science, related discipline, or business administration preferred.

JOB TITLE: **Personnel Representative**

JOB DESCRIPTION: Works in staffing, affirmative action, employee relations, training and development, compensation and benefits, or employee communications.

QUALIFICATIONS: Bachelor's or master's degree in industrial relations, business administration, or behavioral sciences.

JOB TITLE: **Financial Analyst, Management Accountant**

JOB DESCRIPTION: Entry-level accounting jobs usually start at one of HP's divisions and are responsible for product or process cost analysis, financial reporting and forecasting, product profitability and asset evaluation, including inventory and capital equipment. Additional advanced accounting positions handle financial activity for sales regions, product groups, and from the corporate perspective.

QUALIFICATIONS: Most entry-level positions require a master's in business administration.

Intel Corporation
Silicon Valley; Santa Clara

COMPANY PROFILE: Intel is a recognized world leader in four major electronics product areas: semiconductor memory chips, microprocessors, microcomputer systems, and memory systems. The company, which today has some 20,000 employees worldwide, was started in 1968 with thirty-two employees. An initial goal was to reach $100 million in sales within ten years. Intel did it in six. Over the years, Intel has pioneered many new concepts, including silicon gate technology, the world's first 1024-bit dynamic random access memory, the first megabit "bubble" memory, and the microprocessor.

The Santa Clara facility consists of several buildings which house research and development, manufacturing, marketing, and corporate administration functions. You can apply through corporate headquarters in California for professional jobs at any one of Intel's four satellite facilities or apply directly to the outlying area.

HOW TO APPLY: Send resume for professional positions at any location and for hourly positions in Santa Clara to:

> Employment Department
> Intel Corporation
> 2565 Walsh Ave.
> Santa Clara, CA 95051

or apply directly to a satellite facility:

> Employment Department
> Intel Corporation
> 5000 W. Williams Field Road
> Phoenix, AZ 85224
> (Manufacturing and systems development)

> Employment Department
> Intel Corporation
> 4100 Sara Road
> Rio Rancho, NM 87124
> (Components manufacturing)

> Employment Department
> Intel Corporation
> P.O. Box 9968
> Austin, TX 78766
> (Software operations)

Employment Department
Intel Corporation
5200 NE Elam Young Parkway
Hillsboro, OR 97123
(Manufacturing)

How to Follow Up: You'll hear from Intel by mail a couple of weeks after sending your application.

How to Get There: You can walk in to apply, but Intel won't take applications for a position it's not currently hiring for, and it won't grant interviews on the spot.

Prospects: Intel anticipates controlled growth through 1984—hiring mostly experienced, technical people—in addition to continued aggressive college recruitment.

Rewards: In addition to salaries competitive with the industry, Intel offers all its domestic employees the opportunity to grow within the company through an internal job posting system. All job openings are posted for employees before being advertised publicly. The company has organized recreational activities and offers employees discounted tickets to many local events. Employees can take advantage of a stock participation plan for 85 percent of the market value of the stock. And after seven years with the company, all domestic employees are eligible for an eight-week paid sabbatical.

Job Title: **Secretary, Clerk, Word Processor**

Job Description: Supports the technical administration area with a variety of clerical tasks including data entry and word processing.

Qualifications: Minimum 45 words per minute typing and at least a year's experience.

Job Title: **Fab Operator**

Job Description: Works in clean room environment to transfer the intricate electronic circuitry designs to blank silicon wafers by a variety of photographic-like processes.

Qualifications: No previous training or experience required, but plan on extensive on-the-job training.

Job Title: **Technician**

Job Description: Technicians work in a variety of specialties as line maintenance, engineering, process, software, and electronics technicians. All basically perform a variety of technical tasks, including troubleshooting, testing, repairing,

110

and programming basic electronic equipment or products.

QUALIFICATIONS: Two-year associate's degree or equivalent plus one to four years' experience preferred.

JOB TITLE: **Process Engineer**

JOB DESCRIPTION: Develops new processes or new equipment for a specific segment of the manufacturing process such as photomaking, chemical vapor disposition, diffusion, evaporation electrical test, or yield analysis.

QUALIFICATIONS: Bachelor's or master's in electrical or chemical engineering, physics, materials science, or equivalent. Advanced positions require two to five years' experience.

JOB TITLE: **Product Engineer**

JOB DESCRIPTION: Interfaces with customers and internal engineering departments to establish the characterizations of new and existing products and to develop production test programs. Works to improve cost and efficiency of production through testing, packaging, and manufacturing.

QUALIFICATIONS: Bachelor's or master's in electrical engineering or solid state physics. Advanced jobs require two to five years' experience.

JOB TITLE: **Design Engineer**

JOB DESCRIPTION: Designs complex integrated circuits including mass generation, design verification, and test generation of integrated circuits.

QUALIFICATIONS: Bachelor's or master's degree in electrical engineering. Advanced positions require two to five years' experience.

JOB TITLE: **Programmer, Analyst**

JOB DESCRIPTION: Interfaces with Intel user operator and programmer to specify, design, develop, and control various business system programs. Tasks include coding, timing, and documenting business applications.

QUALIFICATIONS: Bachelor's or master's degree in computer science or related field. Advanced jobs require two to five years' experience.

JOB TITLE: **CAD-CAM Engineer**

JOB DESCRIPTION: Develops and enhances software tools used with graphic system data bases.

QUALIFICATIONS: Bachelor's or master's degree in electrical engineering or computer science. Advanced positions require two to five years' experience.

JOB TITLE: **Automation/Robotics Engineer**

JOB DESCRIPTION: Develops electronic and mechanical advanced state-of-the-art assembly and test equipment for Intel components and system manufacturing.

QUALIFICATIONS: Bachelor's or master's degree in electrical or mechanical engineering. Advanced job requires two to five years' experience.

JOB TITLE: **Quality/Reliability Engineer**

JOB DESCRIPTION: Determines failure rates of parts and products, develops reliability screens and reliability programs to ensure high product quality rates. Also offers customer support in service areas.

QUALIFICATIONS: Bachelor's or master's degree in electrical engineering, solid state electronics, device physics, computer science, or materials science. Advanced positions require two to five years' experience.

Litton, Applied Technology

Silicon Valley; Sunnyvale

COMPANY PROFILE: Litton, Applied Technology, a division of Litton Industries, develops and manufactures advanced defense electronic systems for the United States and foreign governments. The company has been a leading supplier of radar warning systems for more than a decade. Other areas of defense expertise are the application of digital computers to real-time electronic warfare systems and nonimaging electro-optics.

HOW TO APPLY: Send resume to:

> Manager, Employment/EEO
> Litton, Applied Technology
> 645 Almanor Ave.
> Sunnyvale, CA 94086

HOW TO FOLLOW UP: The company responds to all applications and resumes by phone or mail in about two weeks. You can call the main number, (408) 773-0777, to be certain your resume was received.

HOW TO GET THERE: You can drop off resumes in person and also check current openings always posted in the Applied Technology front lobby. From Highway 101, take the Mathilda South exit. Go one block to Almanor Avenue, turn right. You'll see Litton, Applied Technology in the first block on your right.

PROSPECTS: In mid-1983 Litton, Applied Technology had 1,800 employees and several long-term contracts which called for expanding personnel. Most jobs are in professional categories rather than production. Occasionally, there are openings for machinists and assemblers, but they need to be highly skilled with experience in defense work. Applied Technology also has an aggressive college recruitment program to bring entry-level engineering and computer science graduates into all areas of the company. They recruit primarily at West Coast schools.

REWARDS: Litton, Applied Technology offers a choice of three medical plans, 100 percent hospitalization insurance, a dental plan, tuition reimbursement, free group life insurance and retirement plan, an eye care program, and a stock purchase plan as part of its benefits package. Everyone works under a flex hour honor system—going to work when they want to between 6:30 and 8:30 every morning.

JOB TITLE: **Systems Engineer**

JOB DESCRIPTION: Analyzes and designs signal processing identification and warning systems.

QUALIFICATIONS: Bachelor's degree in computer, electrical, or systems

113

engineering or the equivalent experience. Experience in theoretical digital design systems and a good knowledge of digital analysis techniques and advanced development research techniques desired.

JOB TITLE: **Scientific Programmer**

JOB DESCRIPTION: Participates in design and implementation of software for computer-based early warning systems. Prepares functional definitions of modules and defines their interaction with each other and with various hardware preprocessing elements.

QUALIFICATIONS: Bachelor's degree in computer science or electrical engineering or equivalent. Need working knowledge of FORTRAN and Assembly language programming plus a familiarity with input/output (I/O) hardware and software.

JOB TITLE: **Computer Systems Test Engineer**

JOB DESCRIPTION: Designs computer interface hardware for system and subsystem testing. Prepares technical reports and software programs for computer testing of printed wiring assemblies.

QUALIFICATIONS: Bachelor's degree in electrical engineering with postgraduate work in computer science or equivalent. Need solid logic background and familiarity with FORTRAN and BASIC computer programming languages.

JOB TITLE: **Receiver Engineer**

JOB DESCRIPTION: Provides technical contributions in the area of wide-frequency-range ECM-related radio frequency receivers. (ECM=electronic counter-measures)

QUALIFICATIONS: Bachelor's degree in electrical engineering or equivalent and knowledge of state-of-the-art components and techniques, their limitations and applied usages. Specifically need knowledge of broad-band crystal video, tunable filters (Yig tuned), and superheterodyne techniques.

JOB TITLE: **Reliability Engineer**

JOB DESCRIPTION: Provides design support in the areas of stress analysis, MTBF predictions, functional and parameter variability analysis, FMECA, failure analysis, and corrective trade-off analysis. (MTBF=mean time between failure; FMECA=failure mode, effects, criticality analysis)

QUALIFICATIONS: Bachelor's degree in electrical engineering or equivalent.

JOB TITLE: **Electro-Optics Engineer**

JOB DESCRIPTION: Performs research and development work on electro-optic devices and systems.

QUALIFICATIONS: Ph.D. in optics or physics or eight to ten years' experience. Need knowledge in electro-optics, acousto-optics, or surface waves (SAW). Experience with device fabrication technology preferred.

JOB TITLE: **Senior Automatic Test Engineer**

JOB DESCRIPTION: Designs hardware interface circuitry and develops software to test complex analog and digital hybrid microcircuits. Responsible for other high level test engineering of new products.

QUALIFICATIONS: Bachelor's degree in electrical engineering or equivalent plus a minimum of five years' experience in automatic test applications, analog and digital circuit design experience plus a knowledge of FORTRAN programming language.

JOB TITLE: **Engineering Process Specialist**

JOB DESCRIPTION: Designs and develops thin-film substrate metallization processes and microelectronic assembly processes in the development and manufacturing of microwave components and state-of-the-art integrated microwave assemblies.

QUALIFICATIONS: At least a bachelor's in chemistry with six to eight years' experience in process engineering including direct experience in several microwave processes. Master's degree or Ph.D. is preferred.

JOB TITLE: **Senior Process Engineer**

JOB DESCRIPTION: Responsible for development and sustaining of assembly processes for complex thick- or thin-film hybrid microcircuits, microwave components, and state-of-the-art integrated assemblies. Works with design and manufacturing engineering teams to solve processing problems in manufacturing.

QUALIFICATIONS: Bachelor's degree in chemistry or materials science or equivalent, plus five years' process engineering experience in semiconductor, hybrid, or microwave component industries.

ROLM Corporation

Silicon Valley; Santa Clara

COMPANY PROFILE: ROLM Corporation was founded in 1969 primarily to design and manufacture field computers fit for rugged environments for military use. Today, with more than 6,000 employees in North America, the company continues to make the military computers in its MIL-SPEC division in San Jose, but also makes telecommunications systems at its corporate headquarters in Santa Clara and at satellite facilities in Austin and Colorado Springs. More than 3,500 people work in Santa Clara where ROLM has corporate headquarters, research and development, and manufacturing facilities. ROLM is a classic new-style company with progressive philosophies based on mutual respect and trust between employer and employee. Everyone in the company enjoys flex hours, profit sharing, participatory management, and opportunities for advancement on the job. The ROLM company's goals are profit, growth, unique products, and a great place to work.

HOW TO APPLY: Send resume to:

> ROLM Corporation
> 4900 Old Ironsides Drive
> Building No.3
> Santa Clara, CA 95050

HOW TO FOLLOW UP: You will get an acknowledgment card after sending your resume and an additional contact from the appropriate department if ROLM wants to interview you. Applications are kept on file for two years. You can call a main number, (408) 986-1000, and ask for Employment to learn the status of your application.

HOW TO GET THERE: ROLM does take walk-in applications, but gives no unscheduled interviews. Heading south from San Francisco, take Highway 101 to Great American Parkway and turn left. Go to Old Glory and turn left again. Bear right at the fork in the road. ROLM is in the first driveway on the left.

PROSPECTS: ROLM has grown at a rapid rate since its founding and expects continued significant growth—but not as fast as its past annual average rate of 50 percent.

REWARDS: Besides the advantages to all employees of the basic corporate lifestyle, the ROLM Santa Clara facility has a $1.5 million recreation center built at the work site. It has racquet ball courts, exercise rooms, swimming pools, jogging track, saunas, and jacuzzis among other amenities. In addition, ROLM offers every employee a three-month sabbatical with pay for every six years worked continuously at the company.

JOB TITLE: **Electrical Engineer—Hardware/Software**

JOB DESCRIPTION: ROLM hires engineers to do four different jobs from this category:

Development Engineer—Does technical design and development of a product.

Production Engineer—Decides how to manufacture a product and solves problems associated with manufacturing.

Product Support Engineer—Determines serviceability and reliability of product; provides technical support to field engineer doing hands-on servicing.

Product Manager—Evaluates market for a product and determines how new products should be packaged and marketed. Each one of the above are members of a team of engineers who may work with a product from research and development (R&D) conception through the product lifetime.

QUALIFICATIONS: Bachelor's or master's in electrical engineering or related engineering discipline. Sometimes product manager also has master's in business administration. ROLM hires both college graduates and engineers with three to five years' experience.

JOB TITLE: **Electronic Technician**

JOB DESCRIPTION: Works in one of the following special areas:

Prototype Technician—Specializes in the building of prototypes for R&D development engineers.

Test Technician—Debugs problems with new products.

Bench Technician—Works as a support technician in manufacturing.

QUALIFICATIONS: Two-year associate's degree in electronics or engineering technology with two to five years' experience.

JOB TITLE: **Assembler**

JOB DESCRIPTION: Operates automated assembly equipment primarily. Some assemblers become highly skilled at repairing mistakes made by automated processes (like removing a misplaced component on a circuit board). ROLM needs relatively few assemblers because of its automation.

QUALIFICATIONS: At least one year's experience, plus must pass hands-on test in basic electronic knowledge including color coding, soldering, and ability to read schematics.

JOB TITLE: **Accountant, Financial Analyst**

JOB DESCRIPTION: Performs host of financial duties including financial analysis and planning, accounting, general ledger, and cost accounting.

QUALIFICATIONS: Bachelor's degree in business administration, finance, or accounting plus experience working as a manufacturing cost accountant. People with master's degrees in business administration, marketing, or finance needed also.

JOB TITLE: **Buyer**

JOB DESCRIPTION: Buys technical parts and components used in ROLM products and not produced in-house.

QUALIFICATIONS: Bachelor's in business administration plus experience in local Silicon Valley vendor pool.

JOB TITLE: **Production Inventory Control Specialist**

JOB DESCRIPTION: Does statistical forecasting and regulates production process in an attempt to produce volume equal to market sales.

QUALIFICATIONS: Bachelor's in business with strong math skills.

JOB TITLE: **Program Analyst, System Analyst**

JOB DESCRIPTION: Writes software programs to make computerized corporate information readily available and usable for short-term and long-term corporate needs.

QUALIFICATIONS: Bachelor's degree in computer science, math, or business plus two to five years' experience, including work on HP 3000 systems.

ROLM, MIL-SPEC Computer Division

Silicon Valley; San Jose

COMPANY PROFILE: This division develops and manufactures military field minicomputers which operate reliably in rugged environments like extremely high and low temperatures. Total employees at this facility in mid-1983 was almost 900.

HOW TO APPLY: Send resume to:

ROLM Corporation
1 River Oaks Place
Mail Stop 230
San Jose, CA 94134

HOW TO FOLLOW UP: You will get an acknowledgment card after sending a resume. Usually, it indicates whether the company is interested in an interview. You can call a main number, (408) 942-8000, and ask for Employment to learn the status of your application.

HOW TO GET THERE: You can apply in person, but not get an interview on the spot. Heading north from San Jose on Highway 101, turn right on the Montague Expressway. Go to North First Street and turn left. Turn left on River Oaks Place (first light), and you'll see ROLM on the corner. The employment office is in Building No. 2.

PROSPECTS: ROLM is in a hiring mode, but mostly for technical people. No applications were being accepted for assemblers in mid-1983, and there were seldom openings for clerical positions.

REWARDS: Employees of the MIL-SPEC division enjoy the same company perks and lifestyle as ROLM employees do corporate-wide. See page 116.

JOB TITLE: **Systems Engineer**

JOB DESCRIPTION: Interfaces between customer and ROLM engineering staff to develop and process new markets and new products.

QUALIFICATIONS: Bachelor's degree in computer science or electrical engineering plus five years' experience with real-time minicomputers and mainframes. Also need knowledge of ROLM products.

JOB TITLE: **Member Technical Staff (MTS)**

JOB DESCRIPTION: Develops software and hardware of new products; plans and implements building and testing of prototypes.

QUALIFICATIONS: Bachelor's degree in computer science or electrical engineer-

119

ing plus software engineers need three to five years' real-time operating or applications software experience.

Syva Company

Silicon Valley; Palo Alto, Cupertino, Mountain View

COMPANY PROFILE: Syva Company (pronounced See-vah) is a subsidiary of Syntex Corporation, an international pharmaceutical company with U.S. headquarters also in Silicon Valley. Syva develops and manufactures diagnostic products ranging from abused drug test kits to computerized hospital and clinical laboratory diagnostic systems. There are three Syva locations in Silicon Valley: administration, corporate headquarters, and research and development in Palo Alto; manufacturing of diagnostic chemistries in Cupertino; and manufacturing of instrument systems in Mountain View.

HOW TO APPLY: Send resume or application to:

> Syva Company
> 900 Arastradero Road
> P.O. Box 10058 Dept. S.H.
> Palo Alto, CA 94303-0847

HOW TO FOLLOW UP: Upon receipt of your application, Syva sends an acknowledgment card to you. Your application is then sent to the appropriate human resources recruiter and hiring supervisor. If they are interested, they call for a personal interview. If not, you will not be notified again, although your application will be kept on file in Human Resources for six months.

HOW TO GET THERE: Syva does accept walk-in applications at its corporate headquarters in Palo Alto. To get there from San Francisco, take Interstate 280 South to the Page Mill exit. Turn left or east on Page Mill and go to Foothill Expressway. Turn right, go to Arastradero Road (second stoplight), turn right. Syva Company is on the corner on the right.

PROSPECTS: Four years ago, Syva employed some 400 people. Today there are 1,200 employees. The annual growth has slowed to a projected 20 percent to 25 percent annually, but there are generally more than twenty pages of current openings posted in the Syva lobby. As with many research oriented companies, there are a great variety of specific job titles, but the categories listed below represent job titles with the largest number of openings.

REWARDS: Besides competitive salaries and benefits, Syva says it offers employees a very positive and participatory work environment. It's a place for the innovative who want creative freedom. Syva says most of the jobs are technical, and in addition to the difficulties of finding technically competent people, they demand people with good interpersonal and communication skills.

JOB TITLE: **Chemist**

JOB DESCRIPTION: There is a wide range of chemist positions at Syva. The basic entry-level chemist job is in manufacturing of diagnostic kits. The products are so precise and the quality concerns so high that most are entirely hand assembled. Many high level chemists are used in research and development, particularly in the areas of biochemistry, protein biochemistry, immunochemistry, and immunology.

QUALIFICATIONS: The minimum requirement for chemists in manufacturing is a bachelor's degree. Many chemists in research and development have Ph.D.'s plus experience in the specialties listed above.

JOB TITLE: **Laboratory Technician**

JOB DESCRIPTION: Technicians assist scientists in all areas from research to manufacturing.

QUALIFICATIONS: Two years of college or associate's degree in one of the sciences, preferably biology or chemistry.

JOB TITLE: **Word Processor**

JOB DESCRIPTION: Word processors are used throughout the company as secretarial support for both administrative and scientific company activities.

QUALIFICATIONS: Minimum two years' word processing experience or equivalent. Syva uses Wang systems, but experience is not required on Wang. Typing skill of at least 60 words per minute is required for lowest level word processor.

122

Hewlett-Packard

San Diego

COMPANY PROFILE: This division of Hewlett-Packard makes graphics plotters, peripheral printers which make hard copies of computer graphics. The plotters are used for everything from pie charts to floor plans, and as a tool in the increasingly popular CAD (computer aided design) systems. The division was created when HP acquired the F.L. Mosley Co. in 1958. Francis Mosley had invented the XY Recorder. In 1968, the division moved to Rancho Bernardo north of San Diego. Today the division does research and development, manufacturing, and marketing at the site. In mid-1983, there were some 1,350 employees.

HOW TO APPLY: Send resume to:

Hewlett-Packard
16399 W. Bernardo Drive
San Diego, CA 92127
Attn: Employment

HOW TO FOLLOW UP: HP sends a letter to acknowledge your application within about three weeks. If there's a potential job match, you'll get another letter or phone call. After three weeks, you can call for the status of your resume to a main number, (619) 487-4100 (ask for Employment).

HOW TO GET THERE: HP takes walk-in applications from 8:30 A.M. to 5:00 P.M. Monday through Friday, but gives no interviews on the spot. From the San Diego airport, take Interstate 5 south to the Escondido exit (Highway 163 North). That becomes Interstate 15 North. Follow Interstate 15 about thirty miles north of San Diego to the Bernardo Center Drive exit. Turn left, and you'll see the shipping entrance for HP on your right side. Follow Bernardo Drive around to the main entrance.

PROSPECTS: Hewlett-Packard in San Diego is in a hiring mode, particularly with the growing use of CAD systems, but most needs are for exempt level personnel.

REWARDS: This division offers all the benefits of HP corporate-wide plus a beautiful Southern California setting. See the Hewlett-Packard write-up earlier in this chapter, page 104.

JOB TITLE: **Development Engineer—Hardware/Software**

JOB DESCRIPTION: As part of research and development design team, works with team and in individual specialty areas to develop new products.

QUALIFICATIONS: Full range of positions from bachelor's, master's, and Ph.D. degrees in electrical engineering, computer science, physics, and/or chemistry with various experience levels.

JOB TITLE: **Process/Manufacturing Engineer**

JOB DESCRIPTION: Works as part of manufacturing team to solve problems and improve the efficiency of the manufacture of an assigned product. Brings new products from research and development (R&D) to manufacturing stage, develops and implements testing and assembly methods, and conducts production cost studies to improve profitability while maintaining and/or improving product quality. Some engineers in this area work as chemists in the production of the pens and paper used on plotters.

QUALIFICATIONS: Full range of positions including bachelor's, master's, and Ph.D. degrees in electrical, mechanical, and industrial engineering, physics, and/or chemistry.

JOB TITLE: **Customer/Product Assurance Engineer**

JOB DESCRIPTION: Works in both R&D and product stages to set product quality performance standards and test for them. Trains and backs up customer service personnel in proper maintenance of HP equipment.

QUALIFICATIONS: Full range of positions including bachelor's, master's, and Ph.D degrees in electrical and mechanical engineering and/or computer science.

JOB TITLE: **Buyer, Scheduler**

JOB DESCRIPTION: Buyer procures materials, components, and services and manages inventories. Scheduler makes sure technical components are in right place at right time in manufacturing process.

QUALIFICATIONS: Bachelor's (master's preferred) in business administration and/or degree in materials science. (HP likes the materials science program at San Diego State.)

JOB TITLE: **Facilities Engineer**

JOB DESCRIPTION: Responsible for entire building facility, including special needs like controlled air conditioning systems in computer rooms, distribution of power systems for electronic operations, and layout and start-up of clean rooms.

QUALIFICATIONS: Bachelor's and/or master's degree in industrial, electrical, or mechanical engineering.

JOB TITLE: **Product Marketing Engineer**

JOB DESCRIPTION: May be assigned to one of the following areas:
 Product Marketing—Uses market analysis to contribute to product definition,

124

stablishes market plan for product, plans and coordinates promotional and sales
fforts, develops sales training programs, including technical literature.

Sales Development and Support—Creates regionally-tailored sales plans, sets
ales quotas, and prepares sales forecasts.

Applications Engineering—Helps develop sales measurement techniques in
xisting and new market areas.

QUALIFICATIONS: Bachelor's degree in electrical or mechanical engineering or
omputer science. Some experience preferred.

JOB TITLE: **Technical Writer**

JOB DESCRIPTION: Writes a variety of technical product and training information
anging from customer technical manuals to brochures and fliers to programming
nanuals.

QUALIFICATIONS: Bachelor's degree in English or journalism with technical
ommunications or computer science course work. Some teachers make good
echnical writers.

JOB TITLE: **Electronics Technician**

JOB DESCRIPTION: Tests product in various stages of development.

QUALIFICATIONS: Two-year associate's degree or equivalent experience. Mili-
ary experience (E5 and above) is good.

COLORADO

From telecommunications to space ships to semiconductors and computers, the Front Range of Colorado is teeming with high-tech companies.

The Front Range is made up of the long strip of cities that stretch along the Rockies between Colorado Springs to the south and Longmont to the north. In between are Denver and Boulder. What used to be open space between metro areas is fast closing up with suburban industrial parks and housing developments.

In the southeast suburbs of Denver—south on Interstate 25—is the Tech Center, a concentration of office parks which house both energy and technology companies. Continuing south about another hour's drive is Colorado Springs, which in a single year was "discovered" by fifteen Silicon Valley companies looking for Sun Belt satellite locations. In mid-1983, the Springs had some thirty-five electronics companies and anticipated some 14,000 new manufacturing jobs by 1985—double the 1983 total.

Aerospace companies are keeping an eye on Colorado Springs too. The planned Consolidated Space Operations Center (CSOC) and a new Air Force Command facility potentially will offer thousands of civilian jobs in addition to the private companies with their space products and support crews.

The Springs, home of the Air Force Academy, had been a sleepy tourist town with lots of retired military before the electronics boom.

To the north along the Front Range there are dozens of start-up entrepreneurial companies—some like Storage Technology Corporation and NBI in the Boulder area which have been classic high-tech success stories.

Hewlett-Packard has major facilities at both ends of the Front Range development—operating divisions in Fort Collins, Loveland, and Greeley to the north and Colorado Springs to the south. HP also recently purchased land for new facilities that could one day employ 16,000 more people.

Colorado fits the engineers' quality of life requirements perfectly. The climate is temperate, the sun shines most of the time, there's plenty of room to grow and, most important, the country's best champagne powder skiing is as close as an hour and twenty minutes.

Summer in the high country is glorious—cool, crisp air, miles and miles of national forest, camping, hunting, hiking, fishing, horseback riding.

The high-tech industry is also perfect for Colorado which has a majority of voters with an environmentalist philosophy that champions the new clean, affluent high-tech industries.

126

American Bell, Engineering, Design, and Development Division (ED&D)

Denver

COMPANY PROFILE: American Bell, ED&D was Bell Laboratories before the Bell System reorganization of January 1, 1983. The company is the marketing subsidiary of AT&T. In the Denver facility, American Bell engineers develop the business communications systems that Western Electric manufactures.

HOW TO APPLY: Send resume to:

American Bell
Engineering, Design, and Development
Division
Technical Employment Department
11900 N. Pecos St.
Denver, CO 80234

HOW TO FOLLOW UP: You will get a response to your resume. If it's positive, you'll get an official application to return and a request for your college transcripts. If you pass that screening, you'll get an interview, travel expenses paid if you're from out of state.

HOW TO GET THERE: Take Interstate 25 north from downtown Denver to the 120th Street exit. Turn left a short distance to Pecos Street. You'll see both Western Electric and American Bell on your left.

PROSPECTS: Depending on needs, American Bell may hire as many as sixty to seventy technical college graduates in the top 10 percent of their class each year. The company also hires experienced professionals with master's and Ph.D.'s and bachelor's degree holders with five to ten years of experience.

REWARDS: American Bell says salaries are competitive and benefits offer a wide variety of plans for well-being and financial stability of employees and their families.

JOB TITLE: **Electrical Engineer, Computer Scientist**

QUALIFICATIONS: Bachelor's or master's degree in electrical engineering or computer science.

JOB TITLE: **Mechanical Engineer**

QUALIFICATIONS: Bachelor's or master's degree in mechanical engineering.

JOB TITLE: Electrical Engineering Technician

QUALIFICATIONS: Two-year associate's degree in electrical engineering technology.

JOB TITLE: Computer Science Technician

QUALIFICATIONS: Two-year associate's degree in computer science technology.

JOB DESCRIPTIONS: The American Bell Laboratory is engaged in the development and design of business communications systems such as PBX's. Most of the high level technical positions above require the ability to apply state-of-the-art system, circuit, and software design and problem-solving techniques to new features and system applications programs. The Lab hires physical designers, circuit designers, electrical engineers, computer programmers, applications programmers, and support personnel. Extensive use is made of computer-based design and documentation aids in providing engineering information functions. Engineering information support services include physical design of circuit boards and cabinetry, circuit pack testing, wiring, art and illustrations, engineering standards, computer program maintenance and updating, and technical documentation.

Ball Aerospace Systems Division

Boulder

COMPANY PROFILE: Ball Aerospace is part of the Ball Corporation (best known for the Ball canning jar). The twenty-five-year-old division is one of the oldest high-technology firms in Boulder. It is one of a handful of American companies that can design and manufacture an entire satellite at its Boulder facility. Ball made history in the 1950s with its revolutionary Orbiting Solar Observatory satellite which took some of the first pictures of the sun from outside the atmosphere. Today, Ball is actively producing one-of-a-kind high-tech products ranging from actuators on the shuttle to highly classified defense systems and subsystems.

HOW TO APPLY: Send resume to:

> Ball Aerospace Systems Division
> Attn: R.D. Shinn
> Dept. 07602
> P.O. Box 1062
> Boulder, CO 80306

HOW TO FOLLOW UP: Ball does respond to all applicants. You can call the employment number, (303) 441-4111 to learn the status of your resume.

HOW TO GET THERE: Ball does accept walk-in applications, but most interviews are by appointment only. From Denver, take the Boulder Turnpike to Foothills Parkway exit. Follow Foothills to Arapahoe Road, turn right. Ball is about a half a mile on your left. Park in the visitors' lot, and walk across the street to the administration building.

PROSPECTS: Ball anticipates aggressive growth in the number of people and revenue over the next five years as the company moves into new product development and new business areas. The company will maintain its role as a prime contractor with NASA and the Department of Defense (DOD) for satellites and instrumentation, but will also expand into some higher volume production of systems and subsystems. Employment in mid-1983 was at about 1,500. Ball says that may as much as double by 1988. Most needs are for highly experienced engineers with special abilities in electro-optical systems, cryogenics, mechanical and antenna engineering. In addition to the mostly technical positions listed below, Ball does hire for administrative positions from time to time, but most require some previous aerospace experience.

REWARDS: In addition to salaries and benefits in line with a Fortune 500 company (which Ball corporation is), Ball offers a tremendous challenge to scientists and engineers who are able to take a product, like a satellite, from the conception of an idea, through the design stage, all the way to the building of a finished product. By maintaining a good mix of contracts, Ball Aerospace Systems Division has also been able to avoid the peaks and valleys resulting in periodic layoffs common to many other aerospace contractors.

JOB TITLE: **Mechanical Design Engineer**

JOB DESCRIPTION: Designs high precision systems or subsystems using special knowledge of cryogenics.

QUALIFICATIONS: Bachelor's and master's degrees in mechanical engineering plus at least five years' experience.

JOB TITLE: **Optics System Design Engineer**

JOB DESCRIPTION: Designs infrared or ultraviolet focal plane arrays.

QUALIFICATIONS: Master's degree (Ph.D. preferred) in electrical engineering, physics, or optics plus at least five years' experience, including work with space flight qualified or DOD system.

JOB TITLE: **Imaging Process Engineer**

JOB DESCRIPTION: Develops software to minimize signal noise from defense image gathering systems.

QUALIFICATIONS: Bachelor's or master's degree in electrical engineering, physics, or computer science plus five years' experience.

JOB TITLE: **Analog/Digital Circuit Design Engineer**

JOB DESCRIPTION: Designs electronics for wide variety of instruments and spacecraft.

QUALIFICATIONS: Bachelor's and master's degree in electrical engineering plus three years' experience.

JOB TITLE: **Control Systems Engineer**

JOB DESCRIPTION: Designs and analyzes state-of-the-art control systems for spacecraft or subsystems. Uses knowledge of Kalman filter system, stability analysis, and closed loop feedback system.

QUALIFICATIONS: Bachelor's and master's degrees in electrical engineering or physics plus five years' experience.

JOB TITLE: **Power Supply Design Engineer**

JOB DESCRIPTION: Designs state-of-the-art low and high voltage power supplies for NASA or military applications. Uses knowledge of linear switching regulators.

QUALIFICATIONS: Bachelor's or master's degree in electrical engineering plus three years' experience.

JOB TITLE: **Packaging Design Engineer**

JOB DESCRIPTION: Designs electronic assemblies from conceptual to detailed mechanical design. Uses knowledge of printer circuits, switch wire welded boards, and wire wrap boards.

QUALIFICATIONS: Bachelor's degree in electrical or mechanical engineering plus five years' experience, including work with NASA or DOD high reliability programs.

JOB TITLE: **Spacecraft Power System Design Engineer**

JOB DESCRIPTION: Designs total electronics system which distributes power to all parts of a spacecraft.

QUALIFICATIONS: Bachelor's degree (master's preferred) in electrical engineering plus five years' experience.

JOB TITLE: **Systems Engineer**

JOB DESCRIPTION: Develops systems concept and translates into hardware requirements. Interfaces between customer and design engineer to help interpret technical requirements of customer. Uses interdisciplinary overview approach to project.

QUALIFICATIONS: Bachelor's and master's degree in engineering discipline plus at least eight years' experience, including knowledge of NASA/DOD requirements.

JOB TITLE: **Antenna Design Engineer**

JOB DESCRIPTION: Does theoretical and detailed hardware designs from concept to product for a wide variety of antennas.

QUALIFICATIONS: Bachelor's, master's, or Ph.D. in electrical engineering and/ or physics plus eight years' experience.

JOB TITLE: **Integrated Circuit (IC) Design Engineer**

JOB DESCRIPTION: Works in the fabrication of GaA (gallium arsenite) microwave monolithic ICs from design through photolithography to implantation, inspection, and testing.

QUALIFICATIONS: Advanced degree in solid state physics or electrical engineering plus at least fifteen years' experience. Secret clearance required.

JOB TITLE: **Program Manager**

JOB DESCRIPTION: Manages a new product from design to development in all aspects from technical, financial, to contractual.

QUALIFICATIONS: Master's degree in engineering or physical science (additional master's in business administration preferred) plus at least ten years' experience including a broad technical program background dealing with NASA or DOD.

JOB TITLE: **Technician**

JOB DESCRIPTION: Works as engineering aide performing many different technical tasks in a wide variety of programs.

QUALIFICATIONS: Two-year associate's degree in electronics plus three to four years' technical experience, preferrably with NASA or DOD programs.

JOB TITLE: **Assembler**

JOB DESCRIPTION: Hand assembles various electronic components and printed circuit boards.

QUALIFICATIONS: Special certification in NASA soldering skills plus experience.

JOB TITLE: **Skilled Machinist**

JOB DESCRIPTION: Performs close tolerance work with hard metals.

QUALIFICATIONS: Seven to eight years' experience.

JOB TITLE: **Programmer**

JOB DESCRIPTION: Works with maintenance and installation of operating system for total data base at Ball Aerospace. Uses knowledge of CICS, VSI, COBOL, System 2000, and JABS.

QUALIFICATIONS: Eight years' experience programming, at least four years with IBM 3031 system.

Coors Porcelain

Golden

COMPANY PROFILE: Coors Porcelain is a subsidiary of the Adolph Coors Company (best known for the brewery). The porcelain division makes some 1,600 different porcelain or ceramic parts for the electronics and other diversified industries, including parts for the brewery's highly automated assembly line operation. The division had more than 2,000 employees in mid-1983 working in Golden and Grand Junction, Colorado, as well as Oregon and some overseas locations.

HOW TO APPLY: Send a resume or application to:

> Coors Placement Center
> 1221 Ford St.
> Golden, CO 80401

HOW TO FOLLOW UP: Coors has a very sophisticated computer system for keeping applications on file, coded by job skills. The company keeps applications active for six months and in 1983 had approximately 40,000 on file. You will get a written response to your application. If you want to know the status of your resume you can call (303) 277-2611.

HOW TO GET THERE: The Coors Placement Center always takes applications and has specific openings posted. Walk-in hours are 7:30 A.M to 4:00 P.M. Monday through Friday. To get there from Denver, take Sixth Avenue west out of Denver and into the foothills. You'll see signs for Golden, and finally, the town of Golden will be on your right. Turn right at a stoplight onto 19th Street, go about a mile to Ford Street and turn left. The employment office is on the corner of 13th and Ford on your right.

PROSPECTS: There are generally openings for technical and professional positions, but Coors does the bulk of its production hiring during the first quarter of every calendar year.

REWARDS: Coors says salaries are competitive with the region.

JOB TITLE: **Electrical Engineer**

JOB DESCRIPTION: Designs industrial systems with an emphasis on power distribution, motor controls, and lighting.

QUALIFICATIONS: Bachelor's degree in electrical engineering plus previous experience.

133

JOB TITLE: **Ceramic Engineer**

JOB DESCRIPTION: Develops processes for alumina oxide, spray drying, ball milling, and body separations.

QUALIFICATIONS: Bachelor's degree in ceramic engineering plus ideally, two years' experience in a ceramics plant.

JOB TITLE: **Chemist**

JOB DESCRIPTION: In charge of supervision, work scheduling, training, and quality assurance in a wet chemical laboratory.

QUALIFICATIONS: Bachelor's degree in chemistry plus four years' experience and/or training in classical wet chemistry (inorganic analytical chemistry).

JOB TIP: Coors has a labor pool (an in-house temporary employment service) which takes applications for a variety of jobs for all of the Coors divisions, including the brewery. Occasionally there are production jobs open in the porcelain division. You apply at the same place and can get up to 1,000 hours of work.

Hewlett-Packard

Fort Collins

COMPANY PROFILE: This HP division, opened in 1976, designs, manufactures, and markets six types of computers designed as aids for engineering. The products can be networked so that teams of engineers can share data files and peripherals from a terminal at each work station.

HOW TO APPLY: Send resume to:

Hewlett-Packard
3404 E. Harmony Road
Fort Collins, CO 80525
Attn: Employment Manager

HOW TO FOLLOW UP: HP sends an acknowledgment letter to each applicant within three weeks. After a review by the proper department manager, you're notified again if the company wants an interview. You can call a main number, (303) 226-3800, and ask for the employment department to learn the status of your application.

HOW TO GET THERE: You can walk in to apply between noon and 4 P.M. Mondays and Fridays only. No interviews are given at that time. HP is accepting applications for all positions, but there are openings mostly for professional jobs. Heading north from Denver on Interstate 25, take the first Fort Collins exit, Harmony Road. Turn left, go about a mile. HP is on the right side of the road.

PROSPECTS: HP in Fort Collins had about 2,300 people in mid-1983 and was experiencing steady growth from the addition of technical people. More automated manufacturing systems and HP's increased buying of pre-assembled components made the outlook dim for hiring additional production workers.

REWARDS: This division enjoys all the benefits offered to HP employees corporate-wide (see page 104) plus at least one special perk in the way of an employee campground. HP Fort Collins owns some 1,500 acres of forest land near Estes Park which employees can use for camping and recreation throughout the year. The company also has a ski club, sailing club, and a variety of planned activities to take advantage of the Colorado High Country.

JOB TITLE: **Development Engineer—Software**

JOB DESCRIPTION: Designs operating and applications software for HP products.

QUALIFICATIONS: Bachelor's degree in electrical engineering, computer science, mathematics, or related discipline and master's degree in computer science with software emphasis.

JOB TITLE: **Production/Fabrication Engineer**

JOB DESCRIPTION: Performs a variety of functions in the process of bringing products from the research and development (R&D) stage to production. Helps determine manufacturing processes, develops and implements test and assembly methods, and determines best techniques and tools for making highest quality products at lowest costs.

QUALIFICATIONS: Bachelor's degree in mechanical, electrical, or industrial engineering. Master's in business administration preferred.

JOB TITLE: **Materials Engineer**

JOB DESCRIPTION: Recommends best parts and vendors and sets up technical parts testing and procurement procedures to meet and improve product requirements.

QUALIFICATIONS: Bachelor's degree in electrical or mechanical engineering. Master's degree in engineering or business administration preferred.

JOB TITLE: **Product Assurance Engineer**

JOB DESCRIPTION: Works in both R&D and manufacturing stages to assure product reliability in areas of thermal and software reliability. Designs and develops automated test systems for those properties.

QUALIFICATIONS: Bachelor's degree in electrical, mechanical, or industrial engineering. Master's degree preferred.

JOB TITLE: **Marketing Engineer**

JOB DESCRIPTION: May be assigned to one of following areas:
Product Marketing—Uses market analysis to contribute to product definition, establishes market plan for product, plans and coordinates promotional and sales efforts, develops sales training programs, including technical literature.
Sales Development and Support—Creates regionally-tailored sales plans, sets sales quotas, and prepares sales forecasts.
Applications Engineering—Helps develop sales measurement techniques in existing and new market areas.
Product Support—Trains and backs up customer representatives and customers in maintenance of HP equipment.

QUALIFICATIONS: Bachelor's degree in electrical engineering, computer science, mathematics, or related discipline. Master's in business administration preferred.

JOB TITLE: **Programmer, Analyst**

JOB DESCRIPTION: At entry level, performs moderately complex computer programming functions, including system documentation and development of test data and routines. Can evolve to project leader responsible for directing systems development and implementation.

QUALIFICATIONS: Bachelor's degree in computer science or related discipline. Master's degree in computer science, related discipline, or business administration preferred.

Honeywell, Inc., Test Instruments Division (TID)
Denver

COMPANY PROFILE: The Honeywell Instruments Division designs, manufactures, and markets instruments for use in industry and government testing. Among its products are magnetic tape processing and recording equipment, signal conditioning equipment, customized military equipment for data recording and display recording, hard copy imaging recorders, data acquisition systems, and computerized recording systems.

HOW TO APPLY: Send resume to:

> Honeywell Test Instruments Division
> P.O. Box 5227
> Denver, CO 80217
> Attn: Employee Relations

HOW TO FOLLOW UP: Honeywell keeps resumes active in search of a job match for a month. If there's an opening the company calls you for an interview. If not, the company sends you a letter telling you so. You're welcome to call during the month for a status report, (303) 773-4695.

HOW TO GET THERE: You can drop off your resume or application between 7:30 A.M. and 4:00 P.M. Monday through Friday in the main lobby. Take Interstate 25 south from Denver to Arapahoe Road. Turn west to Holly. Turn left (south) to Dry Creek Road. Turn right (west), and you'll see Honeywell. The address is 4800 East Dry Creek Road, Littleton.

PROSPECTS: Honeywell has been in this location since 1954. Today there are 1,100 employees (350 in manufacturing), and the company says there is generally some hiring activity, at least for turnover.

REWARDS: Honeywell has supervised flex time at this facility, an in-house cafeteria, and, according to the company, an excellent benefits package. Salaries are very competitive. An entry-level assembler with no experience starts at $6.31 an hour.

JOB TITLE: **Assembler**

JOB DESCRIPTION: There are various levels of assemblers. Entry-level assemblers with no experience work with circuit cards and wiring assemblies.

QUALIFICATIONS: Prospective assemblers must take a manual dexterity aptitude test, given through the Colorado Jobs Service Office at 1330 Fox in Denver. Call the Jobs Service, (303) 866-6464, and ask the Exclusive Accounts Department to schedule you for a test. You'll fill out an employment application when you go for testing.

JOB TITLE: **Electronics Technician**

JOB DESCRIPTION: Performs testing, checking, and inspecting duties.

QUALIFICATIONS: Two-year associate's degree in electronics, minimum. Level at which you're hired depends on experience and score on written test given all applicants.

JOB TITLE: **Engineering Aide**

JOB DESCRIPTION: Works on research and development team as an aide to engineers in development of new products.

QUALIFICATIONS: Minimum two-year associate's degree in engineering. Higher levels need varying levels of experience.

JOB TITLE: **Drafter—Mechanical Design/Computer Aided Design (CAD)/ Electrical**

JOB DESCRIPTION: Does final drafting of engineering roughs for mechanical or electrical product design. Also some drafters work particularly with CAD systems.

QUALIFICATIONS: Two-year associate's degree in drafting with experience in electronics design.

JOB TITLE: **Clerical**

JOB DESCRIPTION: Various jobs ranging from clerk to word processor to executive secretary working in a variety of settings from receptionist to highly technical positions are open from time to time.

QUALIFICATIONS: Minimum typing skill required is 40 words per minute.

JOB TITLE: **Electrical Engineer**

JOB DESCRIPTION: Works as design, manufacturing, or quality engineer.

QUALIFICATIONS: Bachelor's degree in electrical engineering. Full range of positions from entry level (degree only) to three or more years' experience.

JOB TITLE: **Software Engineer**

JOB DESCRIPTION: Works in the design area. Writes application software for new products.

QUALIFICATIONS: Bachelor's degree in electrical engineering or computer science. There are a range of positions from entry level (degree only) to three or more years of experience.

Job Tip: Honeywell hires from two in-house temporary labor pools—one for nonexempt workers like clerical workers, drafters, and engineering aides and the other for hourly jobs like entry-level assembler. You can check a box on your initial application if you're interested in temporary work. Honeywell says it may lead to a full-time position.

Honeywell, Inc.

Colorado Springs

COMPANY PROFILE: Honeywell was the first solid state electronics company to begin manufacturing in Colorado Springs. It opened with fifty people in 1974 and today has more than 700 employees. The company is almost entirely a manufacturing division (wafer fabrication), with minimal design and development. The majority of the manufacturing is in clean room environments—sealed rooms with air constantly circulating to minimize troublesome dust particles.

HOW TO APPLY: For professional positions, send resume to:

> Honeywell, Inc.
> 1150 Cheyenne Mountain Blvd.
> Colorado Springs, CO 80906
> Attn: Personnel

For hourly jobs, you must apply at the Colorado State Jobs Service Office in Colorado Springs. Honeywell uses the state agency to screen hourly applicants. The company posts open jobs there as well.

HOW TO FOLLOW UP: Professional applicants receive an acknowledgment card in a couple of days. Resumes are then referred to the appropriate hiring manager. If there's a potential job match, you're called for an interview; if not, you get a letter telling you. You can call the main number, (303) 576-3300, and ask for a recording which lists current openings or ask for a live person to tell you the status of your resume.

HOW TO GET THERE: Honeywell prefers that professionals send resumes rather than walk in to apply since interviews cannot be arranged on the spot.

Applicants for hourly jobs must go in person to the Jobs Service. To get there, take the Bijou exit off Interstate 25 and turn west (toward the mountains). Go to the second light, turn left on Spruce, and go one block to the Jobs Service office at 17 North Spruce. Hours are from 8 A.M. to 5 P.M. Monday through Friday.

PROSPECTS: Honeywell is hiring on an ongoing basis for the jobs listed below. However, the company says it gets many more applications than it has jobs, particularly for hourly production jobs. It is one of the few companies that maintained its 20 percent to 30 percent annual growth through the recent recession that hit many new Colorado Springs electronics firms.

REWARDS: Salaries for professional jobs are competitive on a national scale, says Honeywell. Production jobs are competitive locally, but the scale is going up with the growth of high tech in the Springs.

JOB TITLE: **Production Operator**

JOB DESCRIPTION: Performs the basic production tasks of wafer fabrication, working in clean room dress and with mostly automated equipment.

QUALIFICATIONS: Honeywell emphasizes this is a semi-skilled job once the company has trained you on the job. (That takes six months.)It's a thinking job that requires dexterity and good eyesight for tasks like alignment of wafers while looking through microscopes.

JOB TITLE: **Electronics Technician**

JOB DESCRIPTION: Keeps the complicated and precise machinery properly maintained and repaired.

QUALIFICATIONS: Two-year associate's degree plus two to three years' experience with wafer fab equipment preferred.

JOB TITLE: **Process Engineer**

JOB DESCRIPTION: Maintains and monitors everything that affects production—yields, chemicals, equipment, processes—in order to constantly upgrade to a more cost efficient, but quality, product. Quality, facility, industrial, and sustaining engineers are also hired in this category to monitor and upgrade a particular aspect of production.

QUALIFICATIONS: Bachelor's degree in electrical engineering minimum. Higher level positions require two to three years' experience.

142

International Business Machines Corporation (IBM)

Boulder

COMPANY PROFILE: IBM's Boulder facility develops and manufactures copiers, copier systems, information distributors, and diskette drives. The Information Distributor combines the technologies of electronic communications, laser printing, and electrophotographic copying in a single product. Diskette drives are used in many IBM products to store data and instructions. The Boulder IBM also produces supplies for copiers. The major technologies used are electrophotography and magnetic media. In the development and production process, Boulder IBM uses lasers, computer aided design (CAD) systems, robotics and automation, VLSI (Very Large Scale Integration) design, and software engineering techniques.

HOW TO APPLY: Send resume to:

> IBM Corporation
> Employment Department
> Building 021
> P.O. Box 1900
> Boulder, CO 80302

HOW TO FOLLOW UP: You will get a written response to your resume, and you'll also be entered in a computerized list under the proper job category for at least six months.

HOW TO GET THERE: You probably can't get an interview on the spot, but you can drop off your application or resume in the Employment Lobby. Coming from Denver, take the Boulder Turnpike (Highway 36) through Boulder to the Diagonal (Highway 119), turn right and go about five and a half miles to IBM on the left side of the road.

PROSPECTS: IBM in Boulder in mid-1983 had some 4,500 employees and anticipated that remaining steady into 1984. The company was taking applications for both hourly and professional positions.

REWARDS: IBM has a nationally competitive salary and benefits package for professional positions. In addition, the company policy is one of full employment, meaning layoffs are rare.

JOB TITLE: **Electrical/Manufacturing Engineer**

JOB DESCRIPTION: Develops and implements processes to improve the manufacturing process—particularly utilizing automated equipment and methods.

QUALIFICATIONS: Bachelor's, master's, or doctorate degree in electrical or manufacturing engineering or equivalent knowledge/experience.

143

JOB TITLE: **Reliability Engineer**

JOB DESCRIPTION: Develops new product design concepts which result in more reliable, service-free products.

QUALIFICATIONS: Bachelor's or master's degree in electrical or mechanical engineering or equivalent knowledge/experience.

JOB TITLE: **Computer Programmer**

JOB DESCRIPTION: Writes new software programs for IBM products.

QUALIFICATIONS: Bachelor's, master's, or doctorate degree in computer science, engineering, or mathematics or equivalent knowledge/experience.

JOB TIP: IBM is becoming more and more interested in people with skills in automation—from engineers to technicians—as the company steps up cost competition by focusing on automating more of its manufacturing processes.

Martin Marietta Denver Aerospace

Denver

COMPANY PROFILE: Martin Marietta in Denver has some 350 contracts for space launch systems, payload integration, command and information systems, space satellites, solar systems, strategic missiles, along with extensive research and development facilities. The biggest projects in mid-1983 were the Titan III and the Peacekeeper (MX). Some 60 percent of Martin Marietta's 9,000 Denver employees are engineers, and a good many more have technical skills.

HOW TO APPLY: Send resume or application to:

> Martin Marietta
> Denver Aerospace
> P.O. Box 179, Mail L1311
> Denver, CO 80201

HOW TO FOLLOW UP: From out of state, you can call a toll-free number, 1-800-525-8846, for jobs information, to request that an application be sent to you, or find out the status of your resume. Within Colorado, call (303) 977-2720. Applications are filed by computer and kept active at least six months.

HOW TO GET THERE: Martin Marietta's main facilities—labs, testing centers, manufacturing areas—are located on 5,100 acres about twenty miles southwest of downtown Denver in the foothills. But unless you're invited, don't make the drive. You won't get past security at the main gate. If you're applying for a nonexempt or hourly job, you can go to Martin's Personnel Staffing Office off the main grounds. From downtown Denver, take Broadway south to Mineral (7900 south), turn right, and go a half mile.

PROSPECTS: Martin Marietta's tremendous growth over the last few years (3,000 new hires in 1981 and 2,000 new hires in 1982) has slowed to about fifty people a month, including new hires and turnover.

REWARDS: Employees are divided into exempt, nonexempt, and hourly worker categories. Salaries and benefits for the first two are competitive with the industry and the area. Hourly workers are all part of the International Union of United Automobile, Aerospace, and Agricultural Implement Workers of America.

EXEMPT JOBS

JOB TITLE: **Engineer—Aerospace/Civil/Computer Science/Electrical/Electronic/Materials/Manufacturing/Mechanical/Quality Assurance/Systems/Systems Safety**

JOB DESCRIPTION: Many engineers are hired each year, usually directly off campuses, to fill entry-level positions in a wide variety of research and development and manufacturing functions relating to product lines. Starting pay differs from discipline to discipline and is dependent on grade point average, school, and related experience. The range is usually between $20,000 and $30,000 a year. Top pay for nonmanagement engineers is $40,000 to $50,000, but 75 percent of Martin's engineers go into management and receive higher pay.

QUALIFICATIONS: Bachelor's, master's, or Ph.D degree in one of the disciplines above.

NONEXEMPT JOBS

JOB TITLE: **Technician—Electronic/Mechanical**

JOB DESCRIPTION: Works as support for engineers in areas of research and development, electronic test equipment, spacecraft, and computer science.

QUALIFICATIONS: Two-year associate's degree plus some experience preferred. Military can be substituted for training and experience.

JOB TITLE: **Draftsman**

JOB DESCRIPTION: Needs electronics drafting abilities more than mechnical.

QUALIFICATIONS: Two-year associate's degree in drafting, two years' experience preferred.

JOB TITLE: **Mathematician, Statistician**

JOB DESCRIPTION: Works in accounting and engineering areas.

QUALIFICATIONS: Some experience, but no formal training required. Simple bookkeeping could qualify you for entry level.

JOB TITLE: **Word Processor**

JOB DESCRIPTION: Performs entry-level word processing duties.

QUALIFICATIONS: Clerical experience preferred. Need at least 50 words per minute on typing test. Word processors were in demand in mid-1983 and could expect overtime.

JOB TITLE: **Secretary**

JOB DESCRIPTION: Performs a variety of clerical duties, some with technical information.

QUALIFICATIONS: Minimum 50 words per minute typing and 60 words per minute shorthand at entry level. Need some clerical experience. Secretaries at Martin are in almost as high demand as engineers.

JOB TITLE: **Quality Control Inspector**

JOB DESCRIPTION: Works in electronics/electrical area inspecting printed circuit boards, in the fabrication area inspecting mechanical machine parts, in the missile assembly area doing both mechanical and electrical inspections, and in shipping and receiving inspecting everything coming in and going out of Martin.

QUALIFICATIONS: Practical experience, usually available only in the aerospace industry.

JOB TITLE: **Machinist**

JOB DESCRIPTION: Needs are in the following areas: lathe operators, milling machine operators, drill press operators, and sheet metal workers. Pay scale is low compared to similar jobs back East (average $6.03 to $8.09 an hour).

QUALIFICATIONS: Skilled tradesman with experience.

JOB TITLE: **Jig and Fixture Builder, Tool and Die Maker**

JOB DESCRIPTION: Martin says these trade positions are hardest to fill.

QUALIFICATIONS: Skilled tradesman with experience.

JOB TITLE: **Electronic Fabricator**

JOB DESCRIPTION: Puts together printed circuit boards as basic entry-level assembly worker. Fabricators are hired in groups of about sixty, two or three times a year and trained to do it the "Martin way."

QUALIFICATIONS: Two years' experience.

JOB TITLE: **Maintenance/Construction/Internal Staff**

JOB DESCRIPTION: Martin says it regularly hires electricians, pipefitters, millwrights, some heating and air conditioning mechanics, janitors, cafeteria workers, and vending machine service representatives to take care of Martin's physical and in-house facilities.

QUALIFICATIONS: Experience required for all jobs.

JOB TIP: Martin Marietta will not pay travel expenses for you to interview or move to Colorado if you're looking for a nonexempt or hourly job. So, the company automatically rejects applications for those jobs from out of Colorado unless you specify that you're willing to travel and relocate at your own expense. You must say that in a letter with your initial application.

NBI, Inc.

Boulder

COMPANY PROFILE: NBI, Inc.'s corporate goal is to become the major, independent manufacturer of high-performance office automation systems in the world. In ten years, the company has grown to some 1,800 employees internationally—about half of them at the Boulder facility. Research and development, manufacturing, and corporate administration offices are housed in a new campus of buildings occupied in early 1983. The company was started developing and producing word processing office products, but in the spring of 1983 added wholly integrated computer office systems, made up of what the company calls ergonomic work stations. They're called ergonomic because the equipment is built with versatility in positioning, etc., to offer the user maximum comfort.

HOW TO APPLY: Send resume to:

> NBI, Inc.
> Box 9001
> Boulder, CO 80301
> Attn: Employment

HOW TO FOLLOW UP: NBI responds to all applications within about six weeks. The letter will indicate whether the company wants an interview. If you haven't heard anything after six weeks, call a main number, (303) 444-5710, and ask for Employment to learn your status.

HOW TO GET THERE: You can apply in person, but there are no unscheduled interviews. Coming from Denver, take the Boulder Turnpike (28th Street) through Boulder to Highway 119 (marked the Diagonal). Turn right, go a half a mile, turn right again on 47th Street. NBI's main entrance is about a half a block. Follow the employment signs.

PROSPECTS: Like many other companies, NBI suffered with the economic recession and in 1983 cut back on its aggressive growth pattern. In mid-1983, the company said it was doing moderate hiring and hoped to pick up speed again in 1984. Needs were particularly to fill technical skilled positions although there was also across-the-board growth in administrative areas. NBI reported particular growth in financial/accounting and product planning areas as well as in technical sales areas. Some hiring was also reported in human resources and training in addition to the technical areas listed below. NBI says it hires 20 percent to 30 percent of its new hires at entry levels out of college or technical school.

REWARDS: In addition to competitive salary and benefits packages, NBI says it offers talented, aggressive people key spots in a fast growing, solid company. NBI says it's looking for overqualified people who can grow quickly with the company's management team.

148

JOB TITLE: **Electrical/Computer Engineer**

JOB DESCRIPTION: Works as part of the design group creating hardware and software for new products.

QUALIFICATIONS: Bachelor's or master's degree in electrical engineering or computer science. Full range of positions from entry level to project manager which requires up to ten years of technical and managerial experience.

JOB TITLE: **Manufacturing Engineer**

JOB DESCRIPTION: Develops, implements, and upgrades automated manufacturing systems.

QUALIFICATIONS: Bachelor's degree in industrial or mechanical engineering, at least three years' experience preferred.

JOB TITLE: **Materials/Purchasing Manager**

JOB DESCRIPTION: Buys all technical parts from outside vendors needed for NBI products.

QUALIFICATIONS: At least three years' experience, engineering degree optional with adequate experience.

JOB TITLE: **Electronic Technician**

JOB DESCRIPTION: Tests product and performs technical assembly of prototypes.

QUALIFICATIONS: Two-year associate's degree in electronics. Full range of positions from entry level to several years' experience.

JOB TITLE: **Assembler**

JOB DESCRIPTION: Performs some soldering and operates automated assembly equipment.

QUALIFICATIONS: No experience, but few openings.

ROLM Corporation

Colorado Springs

COMPANY PROFILE: ROLM has had a manufacturing facility in Colorado Springs since the fall of 1980. It makes computerized business communications systems. The company was in temporary quarters in mid-1983, with plans to move into its own new building by mid-1984.

HOW TO APPLY: Send resume to:

> ROLM Corporation
> 2180 Executive Circle
> Colorado Springs, CO 80906
> Attn: Personnel

HOW TO FOLLOW UP: You will receive a letter acknowledging your application within about three weeks. It usually has an indication of the company's interest. Applications are kept on file for a year.

HOW TO GET THERE: You can apply in person from 8 A.M. to 5 P.M. Monday through Friday, but no interviews are given then. Heading south on Interstate 25 from downtown Colorado Springs, take Circle Drive exit. Turn left onto Circle and then right on Janitel heading south. Take the first left onto Executive Circle.

PROSPECTS: In mid-1983, ROLM had about 135 employees and was projecting a work force of some 300 in 1984. The company's ten-year plan calls for as many as 2,000 people in the Springs facility. There are occasional openings for administrative jobs, but most new hires are in the manufacturing categories listed below.

REWARDS: ROLM offers most facets of the new-style high-tech working environment. All employees have flex hours, good benefits, and after six months everyone becomes eligible for profit sharing and stock purchase plans.

JOB TITLE: **Electronic Assembler**

JOB DESCRIPTION: Performs soldering, wiring, and some mechanical assembly tasks. There are three levels of assemblers, depending on experience and ability.

QUALIFICATIONS: Need good manual dexterity, knowledge of electrical color coding, and one to three years' experience.

JOB TITLE: **Electronics/Test Technician**

JOB DESCRIPTION: Tests printed circuit boards, console parts, and systems.

QUALIFICATIONS: Two-year associate's degree in electronics or equivalent experience. Need knowledge of AC-DC theory, circuit analysis, transistor theory, and digital logic.

JOB TITLE: **Manufacturing/Production Engineer**

JOB DESCRIPTION: Works to improve processing and assembly methods for printed circuit boards.

QUALIFICATIONS: Bachelor's degree in electrical engineering. Experience preferred.

Storage Technology Corporation (STC)

Boulder

COMPANY PROFILE: Storage Technology Corporation is a fourteen-year-old multinational company which develops, manufactures, and services computer data storage equipment and high-speed impact printers. Company founder Jesse Aweida has announced plans to move from the manufacture of peripheral devices only to broad-based computer mainframes by 1984. That kind of aggressiveness has made STC among Colorado's best prospects for job hunters—in 1978 alone the company hired 3,500 new employees. The economy caught up with STC in early 1983, and the company was forced to layoff several hundred, but a number had been recalled by mid-year, and employment at the Colorado facility was stable at about 8,000.

HOW TO APPLY: Send resume to:

> Storage Technology Corporation
> Attn: Employment, Mail Drop 29
> 2270 S. 88th St.
> Louisville, CO 80028

HOW TO FOLLOW UP: Resumes are stored in a computer by job skills. If you're called for an entry-level job interview, you'll have to get to STC yourself. If you're a qualified professional, you'll get excellent treatment—including airfare, lodging, and dining if you're from out of state. STC also picks up relocation expenses if you're hired.

To check the status of your resume, you can call the employment office, (303) 673-5300.

HOW TO GET THERE: You can apply in person during business hours Monday through Friday. The company is between Boulder and Denver off the Boulder Turnpike, Highway 36. From Denver, take Interstate 25 north to the Turnpike and go about twelve miles to the Superior exit. Turn right onto a county road with a sign pointing to Louisville. Take the first right off the county road and it will lead you to STC. Employment office is in Building No. 3.

PROSPECTS: There are generally openings at all levels although it may be slow until 1984 when new product lines are into full production.

REWARDS: Some of the entry-level positions like assembler, pay low to start (roughly $4.70 an hour), but the chances for company training and promotions from within are very good. STC is competitive in its professional salaries—entry-level engineers fresh out of school start at $25,000 a year.

JOB TITLE: Assembler

JOB DESCRIPTION: Hand solders components on circuit boards according to schematics.

QUALIFICATIONS: No previous experience necessary, but if you have it, experience in optics is preferred. Manual dexterity required, but no skills test. On-the-job training lasts several weeks.

JOB TITLE: Electronics/Mechanical Technician

JOB DESCRIPTION: Performs product and component testing and does some diagnostic work.

QUALIFICATIONS: Two-year vocational school in electronics or mechanical technician course study. Experience with optics preferred.

JOB TITLE: Programmer

JOB DESCRIPTION: Writes business applications programs for internal use at STC in the areas of manufacturing, business, and finance.

QUALIFICATIONS: At least four years' experience, including knowledge of COBOL and DEC or IBM large mainframes.

JOB TITLE: Systems Analyst

JOB DESCRIPTION: Acts as a liaison between company in-house users of data base systems and programmers in the development of new programs.

QUALIFICATIONS: Bachelor's degree (may be in computer science) plus four to six years' experience working as systems analyst.

JOB TITLE: Engineer—Electrical/Mechanical/Computer Science/Software

JOB DESCRIPTION: Electrical engineer works in analog/digital LSI (large scale integration) design and reads/writes circuit design.
   Mechanical engineer works in head, servo, and fly height design and with HDA (head disk assembly).
   Computer science/software engineer works with microcode and MVS (machine virtual system).

QUALIFICATIONS: Bachelor's or master's degree in electrical or mechanical engineering or computer science plus at least four years' experience.

153

Western Electric
Denver

COMPANY PROFILE: Western Electric makes customer premises switching equipment (business communication systems). The company in mid-1983 employed some 2,600 people. Production workers are union, members of the International Brotherhood of Electrical Workers (IBEW).

HOW TO APPLY: Send resume to:

Western Electric
Attn: Personnel
1200 W. 120th Ave.
Denver, CO 80234

HOW TO FOLLOW UP: Resumes are kept on file indefinitely. You can write for a status on yours if you haven't heard anything.

HOW TO GET THERE: Western Electric technically does not take walk-in applications for jobs it's not hiring for at the moment. You can drop off a resume, however, and your name will go in their files for the future. To get there from Denver, take Interstate 25 north to the 120th Street exit. Turn left to Huron Street, and you'll see the huge Western Electric building on your left.

PROSPECTS: Western Electric was in a downturn with the national economy in 1981 and 1982. The company had laid off hundreds of production workers—assembly, wiring, and testing workers. As of mid-1983, however, most had been recalled, and the employment levels were at least stable. Only top technical people were in demand, however.

REWARDS: Salaries for professionals are dependent on experience and academics and are competitive with a national job market because Western Electric is a national company.

JOB TITLE: **Electrical Engineer**

JOB DESCRIPTION: Directs and performs various engineering testing procedures on communications equipment.

QUALIFICATIONS: Bachelor's degree in electrical engineering with a minimum 3.5 grade point average from ABET (Accrediting Bureau of Engineering Technology) accredited institution.

JOB TITLE: **Computer Software Specialist**

JOB DESCRIPTION: Develops operating software for business communications systems.

154

QUALIFICATIONS: Bachelor's degree in computer science with minimum 3.5
grade point average from ABET accredited institution or equivalent.

FLORIDA

Sunshine is one of the biggest reasons high-tech companies are going to Florida. They're settling in locations all over the state, but one of the leading concentrations of growth is in the Tampa-Clearwater area. The vast urban area on the Gulf side of the Florida peninsula is made up of the major cities of Tampa, Clearwater, and St. Petersburg and encompasses surrounding development in Pinellas and Hillsborough Counties.

Over the last eight years, the area has added more than 2,000 new jobs a year in high tech.

The area used to be predominated by agriculture and the tourist industry. Today, the county extension agent says his job has evolved from advising farmers to helping people keep their lawns in order.

Honeywell and Sperry each have two large facilities there. GTE, General Electric, ECI (a division of E-Systems), Square D Company, Westinghouse, and United Technologies are all open as well.

Paradyne, a homegrown Florida computer company, started twelve years ago in rented space over a beauty shop and today has 3,000 employees working with a highly automated electronic assembly operation.

The University of Southern Florida and some excellent vocational schools supply much of the high-tech talent in the area. In fact, Pinellas Vocational Technical Institute is so good at turning out technicians that a number of large Dallas companies recruit there.

New housing developments are springing up all around the water inlets of Tampa Bay. Houses are situated so that boats can be tied in backyard inlet slips. Tropical flowers and citrus fruit trees bloom through winter. Dozens of golf courses operate the year around.

And finally, there are miles and miles of white sand Florida beaches complete with tropical gulf breezes.

Honeywell Avionics Division

Clearwater

COMPANY PROFILE: Honeywell Avionics Division, with more than 3,500 employees, designs and manufactures guidance, navigation, and control systems and devices for both manned and unmanned space vehicles, ships, submarines, space boosters, tactical and strategic missiles, and precision aircraft. The company's product line also includes communication control/test systems and devices, avionics digital computers, plated wire memories, and hybrid microelectronics. The Clearwater division, part of Honeywell Corporation headquartered in Minneapolis, also does extensive research and development of various advanced technologies for both military and commercial customers.

HOW TO APPLY: Send resume to:

> Honeywell Avionics
> 13350 U.S. Highway 19 South
> Clearwater, FL 33546
> Attn: Employee Relations 120-1

HOW TO FOLLOW UP: Everyone who applies does receive a written response from Honeywell. If you want to find out the status of your resume, you can call (813) 531-4611, ext. 2514. If Honeywell's interested in you, they pay your way to visit the facility.

HOW TO GET THERE: Honeywell accepts walk-in applications and resumes in the Employment Lobby from 8 A.M. 'til noon Monday through Friday. From Tampa International Airport, take Highway 60 toward Clearwater about fifteen miles until you come to Highway 19. Make a left turn (south) on Highway 19 and go about six miles. You'll see Honeywell on your right. The employment office is in Building No. 1.

PROSPECTS: Honeywell doesn't anticipate great numbers of new hires until the economy picks up (they estimate 1985). However, there are openings for a few mechanical and electrical engineers, as well as some administrative positions. The job titles listed below represent at least some potential activity in turnover hiring.

REWARDS: Company spokesmen say benefits and salaries at Honeywell are "very competitive" both in the Florida area and nationally in the electronics field. Benefits include stock option plans; IRAs; health, dental, and life insurance plans; and tuition refunds for approved further education.

JOB TITLE: **Assembler**

JOB DESCRIPTION: Assembles and tests subassemblies required in the fabrication of gyros, accelerometers, circuit boards, and related devices.

QUALIFICATIONS: High school plus forty-hour NASA certified in-plant soldering school.

JOB TITLE: **Inspector**

JOB DESCRIPTION: Performs routine visual, electrical, and mechanical checks on parts and assemblies.

QUALIFICATIONS: High school plus sometimes soldering certification required.

JOB TITLE: **Electronic Technician**

JOB DESCRIPTION: Assembles, calibrates, repairs, and troubleshoots electronic, electrical, and electro-mechanical assemblies.

QUALIFICATIONS: Completion of electronics curriculum at accredited technical or military school. Course work should cover digital electronics including electronic fundamentals, binary math, boolean algebra, and digital logic application.

JOB TITLE: **Mechanical Technician**

JOB DESCRIPTION: Assembles, calibrates, troubleshoots, and repairs precision components related to the final building of gyros and accelerometers.

QUALIFICATIONS: High school plus at least 1,200 hours in watchmaking, instrument repair, or related trades training. Should be able to read schematics, blueprints, wiring diagrams, etc.

JOB TITLE: **Engineering Technician—Electronic/Mechanical**

JOB DESCRIPTION: Builds and tests electronic and/or electro-mechanical assemblies and subassemblies.

QUALIFICATIONS: High school plus appropriate science courses, and vocational school or two-year associate's degree.

JOB TITLE: **Engineering Aide—Electronic/Mechanical**

JOB DESCRIPTION: Assists engineers and technicians in compiling data, preparing technical charts, computing data and statistics, and troubleshooting.

QUALIFICATIONS: Same as engineering technician.

JOB TITLE: **Drafting Technician**

JOB DESCRIPTION: Prepares drawings with instruction from engineering staff for choice of materials, dimensions, tolerances, and standards.

QUALIFICATIONS: Same as engineering technician plus some drafting technicians need experience with CAD-CAM (using computers to convert engineering schematics).

JOB TITLE: **Typist**

JOB DESCRIPTION: Basic entry-level clerical position.

QUALIFICATIONS: Must type 55 words per minute and have good communication skills.

JOB TITLE: **Secretary**

JOB DESCRIPTION: Types and takes shorthand plus general office duties.

QUALIFICATIONS: Must type 55 words per minute, take shorthand at 80 words per minute, plus have good communications skills.

JOB TITLE: **Planning and Control Clerk**

JOB DESCRIPTION: Prepares performance data for financial and engineering planning.

QUALIFICATIONS: Experience in the above plus typing skills.

JOB TITLE: **Junior Publications Typist**

JOB DESCRIPTION: Types technical documents.

QUALIFICATIONS: Needs experience in technical typing and a strong English background.

JOB TITLE: **Cost Control Clerk**

JOB DESCRIPTION: Does day-to-day bookkeeping and monitors project budgets.

QUALIFICATIONS: Needs typing and office skills plus specialized courses in bookkeeping and commercial subjects.

JOB TITLE: **Administrative Assistant**

JOB DESCRIPTION: Assists supervisors in monitoring and reporting department or program expenditures.

QUALIFICATIONS: Bachelor's degree in business.

JOB TITLE: **Production Coordinator**

JOB DESCRIPTION: Coordinates work flow in accordance with promise dates, material arrival dates, build area capacity, and availability of requisite parts.

QUALIFICATIONS: Bachelor's degree in business.

JOB TITLE: **Program Planner**

JOB DESCRIPTION: Prepares charts, graphs, and schedules to show planned time schedule and progress to assure timely completion of projects.

QUALIFICATIONS: Bachelor's degree in business.

JOB TITLE: **Junior Accountant**

JOB DESCRIPTION: Does a variety of accounting functions including establishing journal entries, maintaining property ledgers and documents, computing depreciations, and reviewing ledger and voucher distribution.

QUALIFICATIONS: Bachelor's degree in business.

JOB TITLE: **Development Engineer**

JOB DESCRIPTION: Develops new products that meet performance specifications and modifies existing products according to customer requirements.

QUALIFICATIONS: Bachelor's degree in electrical engineering, mechanical engineering, or computer science.

JOB TITLE: **Design Engineer**

JOB DESCRIPTION: Designs circuits, devices, and/or systems and works with other engineering teams to be certain specifications, product cost, engineering investment, and objectives are reached.

QUALIFICATIONS: Bachelor's degree in electrical engineering, mechanical engineering, or computer science.

JOB TITLE: **Production Engineer**

JOB DESCRIPTION: Applies state-of-the-art assembly and manufacturing techniques to existing production processes, prepares procedural layouts of different operations, and affects design changes to improve productivity.

QUALIFICATIONS: Bachelor's degree in industrial engineering.

International Business Machines Corporation (IBM), Information Network Development and Operation Center

Tampa

COMPANY PROFILE: IBM's Information Network Development and Operation Center in Tampa is responsible for development, operation, and maintenance of a data network to provide services to IBM customers throughout the U.S. The center had around 550 employees in mid-1983. The network allows customers to use applications and productivity tools in Tampa for program development, end-user applications, and data based inquiries as well as providing connections and network management services between customer terminals and processors. A variety of operating systems, programming languages, and end-user applications are used.

HOW TO APPLY: Send resume to:

IBM Corporation
Central Employment
3407 W. Buffalo Ave.
Tampa, FL 33624

HOW TO FOLLOW UP: IBM responds to all applicants by mail. Applicants are asked not to telephone or visit IBM to check on their status.

HOW TO GET THERE: Walk-in applications are accepted but interviews normally are not given at the time of application. The Central Employment Office is located on the corner of Himes and Buffalo Avenues in Tampa Bay Park, which is diagonally across from Tampa Bay Stadium.

PROSPECTS: Limited hiring opportunities. Most professionals are hired off college campuses.

REWARDS: IBM says employee benefits and compensation programs are among the finest in industry. A merit pay system is used—advancement based on performance.

JOB TITLE: **Computer Scientist**

JOB DESCRIPTION: Involved in design, program development, systems installation, and performance analysis with data networks, control programming, subsystems, and access methods.

QUALIFICATIONS: Bachelor's or master's degree in computer science, mathematics, or engineering or equivalent knowledge/experience.

MASSACHUSETTS

"America's Technology Highway" reads the sign as you pull onto the famed Route 128. The companies lining the embankments on either side tell why. In a matter of miles, you see Polaroid, Magnetic Corporation of America, Helix, Safeguard Data Processing, GTE, Digital Equipment, and IBM.

The golden horseshoe, as Route 128 is called, rings the city of Boston and represents a high-tech development area as old, as respected, and as populated by companies and jobs as Silicon Valley. Like the California site's synergism with Stanford, Massachusetts' high tech grew out of Massachusetts Institute of Technology (MIT).

But the lifestyle in the Boston area is different from California. The engineers who work there live in wooded New England suburbs where you see old mansions restored from the 1700s and signs posted to trees reading "Honey for Sale." There are lots of lakes and rolling woods of maple, birch, and pine. At the core is Boston, a bustling traditional Eastern city, a stark contrast to the emerging Austins and Colorado Springs.

The closest resemblance to the Sun Belt boom towns is an area developing in a second ring around the city, Route 495. There the new-style corporate philosophies like that at Data General prevail.

High tech started in the Boston area in the mid-1950s with about thirty companies—mostly in the defense and telecommunications business. Today some 250,000 people work in high tech there. Software and medical technology companies have joined defense as the larger employers.

The Massachusetts High Technology Council, with offices in Boston, is supported by more than a hundred area high-tech companies. One of its primary goals is to improve education in the state to prepare people for the new world of work.

Data General Corporation

Boston—Southboro

COMPANY PROFILE: This Data General facility is the company's oldest manufacturing location. It's primarily responsible for the mechanical assembly of Data General's ECLIPSE series of super minicomputers and some manufacturing of cables.

HOW TO APPLY: Send resume or application to:

Data General
Route 9
Southboro, MA 01772

HOW TO FOLLOW UP: Applications are filed by your area of expertise, and you're notified if you qualify to interview for an opening.

HOW TO APPLY: You can apply in person. This facility is located on Route 9 East in Southboro.

PROSPECTS: Southboro had some 1,200 employees in mid-1983 and anticipated steady growth through 1984. Most openings are for the positions listed below. There are seldom openings for assemblers or entry-level technicians.

REWARDS: Same as Data General employees corporate-wide. See the listing for Data General later in this chapter, page 164.

JOB TITLE: **Electronics Engineer**

JOB DESCRIPTION: Works as quality control and manufacturing engineer.

QUALIFICATIONS: Bachelor's degree in electrical or mechanical engineering. Full range of positions from entry level (degree only) to years of experience.

JOB TITLE: **Secretary, Word Processor**

JOB DESCRIPTION: Performs general clerical duties in various level jobs.

QUALIFICATIONS: Minimum 35 words per minute typing, preferably six months to a year's experience.

Data General Corporation

Boston—Westboro

COMPANY PROFILE: Data General is a fifteen-year-old company with some 15,000 people working worldwide. Ed deCastro, formerly a chief design engineer for Digital Equipment Corporation and still today Data General's chief executive officer, founded the company in an abandoned beauty parlor, selected for its abundance of electrical outlets. (They used hair dryers to heat test circuit boards.) Today Data General designs, manufactures, markets, and services general purpose computer systems. The basic target markets are in the areas of office automation, industrial automation, small business systems, and professional computing. The company has shipped more than 125,000 computer systems. Corporate headquarters, the major research and development facility, and corporation manufacturing functions (purchasing, planning, etc.) are located in Westboro, Massachusetts, around Route 495 circling Boston.

HOW TO APPLY: Send resume to:

> Data General
> 4400 Computer Drive
> Westboro, MA 01580
> Attn: Personnel

HOW TO FOLLOW UP: Although this facility was receiving several thousand applications a week in mid-1983, spokesmen said the company attempts to acknowledge each one. Later, applicants are contacted again if the appropriate company manager wants an interview. If you haven't heard anything positive in a couple of months, you can send another resume.

HOW TO GET THERE: You can walk in to apply, but no interviews are given then. From the Boston area, take Route 9 west to the Flanders Road exit. Turn right on Computer Drive, and you'll see Data General on your left.

PROSPECTS: Data General was in an aggressive hiring mode in mid-1983. The company anticipated adding as many as 1,500 to 2,000 new employees in 1984. In the Westboro facility the company planned to continue to maintain a high investment in research and development personnel. There are three levels for engineers ranging from individual contributor to project leader to management. All levels are hired in the areas listed below. Once at Data General, as an engineer, you can follow a career track either in management or technical areas and expect comparable rewards.

REWARDS: Despite its growth, Data General has retained its original relaxed corporate culture. All employees are considered equal. There's no executive dining room or reserved parking. An open door management policy is a reality.

The dress code, if any, is informal. The company tries to maintain an environment that lends itself to productivity. The entire company—including its satellite facilities—operates with flex hours.

JOB TITLE: **Electrical Engineer**

JOB DESCRIPTION: These engineers, hired from entry level to experienced, design new products in one of the following areas of specialty: systems architecture, CPU (central processing unit) design, logic design, microcode design, peripheral development (mass storage tapes and disks), sensor input/output, distributed systems development, networking and communications, diagnostics, CAD-CAM (computer aided design—computer aided manufacturing) or electromagnetics.

QUALIFICATIONS: Bachelor's or master's in electrical engineering plus experience for higher level positions.

JOB TITLE: **Software Engineer**

JOB DESCRIPTION: Develops software for the following areas: office automation, operating systems, data base management, scientific languages and tools, compiler development, distributed systems, networking development, and CAD-CAM.

QUALIFICATIONS: Bachelor's or master's degree in computer science, experience required for advanced positions.

JOB TITLE: **Development Technician**

JOB DESCRIPTION: Supports prototype development by assembly and testing.

QUALIFICATIONS: Two-year associate's degree in electronics, experience usually preferred.

JOB TITLE: **Product Marketing Specialist**

JOB DESCRIPTION: Identifies products for development which both fit into Data General's business plan and through research are determined to be marketable. Uses research of market including competitive products to do technical strategic planning. Second major position in this area develops market penetration plans for new products.

QUALIFICATIONS: Most positions require a bachelor's in electrical engineering or computer science with a master's in business administration. Also need technical marketing experience in the computer or electronics industries.

Hewlett-Packard

Boston

COMPANY PROFILE: This Hewlett-Packard division, like one in Andover, designs and manufactures medical instruments and monitoring devices. In mid-1983, it had some 1,365 employees.

HOW TO APPLY: Send resume to:

Hewlett-Packard
175 Wyman St.
Waltham, MA 02254
Attn: Personnel

HOW TO FOLLOW UP: Hewlett-Packard acknowledges all resumes within a couple of weeks, then contacts you for an interview if there's a job match. To find out the status of your resume, you can call a main number, (617) 890-6300, and ask for the employment group.

HOW TO GET THERE: HP can't give interviews on the spot, but you can drop off your resume in the main lobby. Coming from Boston on the Mass Turnpike, take Route 128 north. Exit at Wyman Street. You'll see HP straight ahead.

PROSPECTS: In mid-1983, HP anticipated hiring only for exempt or professional positions—primarily those listed below. A freeze was on hiring hourly manufacturing employees.

REWARDS: See details of the HP corporate lifestyle outlined in the corporation profile in Silicon Valley, page 104.

JOB TITLE: **Marketing Engineer**

JOB DESCRIPTION: May be assigned to one of the following areas:

Product Marketing—Uses market analysis to contribute to product definition, establishes market plan for product, plans and coordinates promotional and sales efforts, develops sales training programs, including technical literature.

Sales Development and Support—Creates regionally tailored sales plans, sets sales quotas, and prepares sales forecasts.

Applications Engineering—Helps develop sales measurement techniques in existing and new market areas.

Product Support—Trains and backs up customer representatives and customers in maintenance of HP equipment.

QUALIFICATIONS: Bachelor's degree in engineering or related scientific discipline. Master's degree preferred.

JOB TITLE: **Development Engineer**

JOB DESCRIPTION: Works with design team to research and develop new products.

QUALIFICATIONS: Bachelor's degree in electrical engineering, computer science, or related discipline.

JOB TITLE: **Technical Writer**

JOB DESCRIPTION: Prepares user operating instructions for complex electronic equipment.

QUALIFICATIONS: Bachelor's degree in technical area like electrical engineering or computer science plus at least two years' experience.

NEW MEXICO

In the past, it hasn't been unusual for people to ask whether they needed a passport to travel to New Mexico.

The fact is the city of Albuquerque is no farther south than Los Angeles and no farther west than Denver. A lot more people are finding out where it is because the high-tech industry has discovered it in the last couple of years.

At least five satellite facilities—of Sperry, Intel, Motorola, Signetics, and Honeywell—are open and hiring in Albuquerque. They came, they say, for the quality of life.

Albuquerque is built along the Rio Grande river basin surrounded by mile-high mesas and the 10,600-foot Sandia Mountain. The climate is mild—average winter midday temperatures are in the fifties.

The original city was founded as a Spanish villa in 1706. That core is preserved in Albuquerque's popular Old Town today—a delightful group of art galleries, craft shops, and restaurants surrounding a town plaza dominated by the San Felipe de Neri Church. The Southwestern flavor is evident throughout the city and the state, especially in Sante Fe and Taos, the popular tourist attractions north of Albuquerque.

The other selling point for the Albuquerque area is the strong base of technical people. Some 17,000 people, many engineers with Pd.D.'s, work at Los Alamos National Laboratories about ninety miles from Albuquerque. The Air Force's White Sands Missile Range is about 150 miles away. And Sandia National Laboratories is on the outskirts of the city. The University of New Mexico rounds out the academic foundation.

In addition, Albuquerque supports three ballet companies as one facet of its cultural offerings.

Sandia National Laboratories

Albuquerque

COMPANY PROFILE: Located on Kirtland Air Force Base on the southeast edge of Albuquerque, Sandia National Labs is primarily involved with research and development, including nuclear weaponry. Sandia was opened in 1945 and is a subsidiary of Western Electric. The labs operate as a service to the U.S. Government at no fee and no profit. The Department of Energy uses Sandia as a prime contractor for various national security and energy projects. Only research and development is done there. Manufacturing is contracted elsewhere.

HOW TO APPLY: Send resume to:

> Staff Recruiting and Employment
> Division #3531
> Sandia National Laboratories
> Box 5800
> Albuquerque, NM 87185

HOW TO FOLLOW UP: Sandia acknowledges receipt of all resumes within a reasonable time.

HOW TO GET THERE: Sandia does not encourage walk-in applications.

PROSPECTS: Sandia has some 8,000 employees—nearly 7,000 in Albuquerque and 1,000 at another facility in Livermore, California. Employee turnover is unusually low. Nearly all employees have technical backgrounds. A Ph.D. is required for physical science backgrounds and either a master's or Ph.D. for engineering.

REWARDS: Salaries and benefits are on par with the national high-tech market.

JOBS: Sandia has people on its staff from virtually all engineering and physical science backgrounds.

Signetics Corporation

Albuquerque

COMPANY PROFILE: This manufacturing facility of the Silicon Valley-based Signetics Corporation, makes MOS (metal oxide silicon) circuits. Signetics in Albuquerque has been open since April of 1982.

HOW TO APPLY: Send resume to:

> Signetics Corporation
> 9201 Pan American Freeway NE
> Albuquerque, NM 87184
> Attn: Employment

HOW TO FOLLOW UP: The company responds to all applications after the appropriate department manager has screened them—usually within a month. If there's no immediate job match, Signetics keeps your application in an active file for six months.

HOW TO GET THERE: You can apply in person, but there are no unscheduled interviews. Take Interstate 25 north from downtown Albuquerque to the east Tramway exit. Go under the freeway and turn left on the west frontage road. Go about a mile, and you'll see Signetics.

PROSPECTS: The Albuquerque facility of Signetics started with 35 employees and had 350 in mid-1983. The number was expected to reach some 600 by the end of 1984.

REWARDS: In addition to California-scale salaries and benefits, Signetics offers a work environment of strong teamwork. Participatory management, along with an emphasis on quality, are part of every employee's work life. In keeping with the company's commitment to promotion from within, all open jobs are posted for existing employees before outside hiring is begun.

JOB TITLE: **Wafer Fab Operator**

JOB DESCRIPTION: Works in various capacities in the front end operation of silicon chip making.

QUALIFICATIONS: No previous wafer experience. Company trains for at least ninety days. Need correct color vision and qualities of neatness and thoroughness (as indicated by appearance and completeness of application).

JOB TITLE: **Line Maintenance Technician**

JOB DESCRIPTION: Works either in front- or back-end operation to maintain automated equipment.

QUALIFICATIONS: Two-year associate's degree in electronics.

JOB TITLE: **Process Engineer**

JOB DESCRIPTION: Works in wafer fab area to improve and maintain product quality and yield.

QUALIFICATIONS: Bachelor's or master's degree in electrical or chemical engineering, or physics, chemistry, or materials science. Some with associate's degree in technical science qualify. Full range of positions including entry level, but at least one year's experience preferred.

JOB TITLE: **Product Engineer**

JOB DESCRIPTION: Has total knowledge of product in order to follow it through manufacturing and troubleshoot problems.

QUALIFICATIONS: Bachelor's or master's degree in electrical engineering plus one year's experience preferred.

JOB TITLE: **Systems Programmer**

JOB DESCRIPTION: Sets up computerized systems for manufacturing, including testing and fabrication, statistical analysis, and data gathering.

QUALIFICATIONS: Bachelor's degree in computer science or computer engineering.

Sperry

Albuquerque

COMPANY PROFILE: This division of Sperry (formerly referred to as Sperry Flight Systems) is a defense contractor that designs and manufactures electronic flight control devices and systems. This facility opened in early 1981 as an outgrowth of other Sperry flight systems divisions headquartered in Phoenix. Sperry in Albuquerque had some 1,000 employees in mid-1983. About 75 percent of the company's products are "black boxes"—literally black boxes about 18-by-8-by-12 inches which contain intricate electronic systems to operate various controls of military aircraft. Because of the defense work, all employees need to be U.S. citizens, and many need to get security clearances after hired.

HOW TO APPLY: Send resume to:

> Sperry
> Box 9200
> Albuquerque, NM 87119
> Attn: Employment

HOW TO FOLLOW UP: Sperry acknowledges all resumes in two to three weeks, requesting an interview if there's a current job match. Resumes are kept on file for six months. You can call a recorded hotline, (505) 821-3726, for current employment information, or (505) 822-5021 for information on the status of your application.

HOW TO GET THERE: Sperry takes walk-in applications only for jobs which have current openings. To get to the employment office, take Interstate 25 north from Albuquerque to the Osuna exit. Go left to the west frontage road, turn right, and continue north to San Diego Street. Turn left on San Diego Street and go about a half mile. You'll see the Sperry parking lot ahead.

PROSPECTS: Sperry is in a strong growth mode in order to fulfill defense contracts the company has now. Projections call for hiring 1,500 to 2,000 additional people in the next three to five years—the majority in professional positions.

REWARDS: Besides competitive salaries and benefits, Sperry says it offers the excitement of growth with strong individual opportunities for talented, skilled employees. Sperry describes its work environment as a professional atmosphere with top engineers, but not stuffy. Sperry's new-style work environment, including an open door management policy, is epitomized by the company motto: "We Listen."

JOB TITLE: **Digital/Analog Design Engineer**

JOB DESCRIPTION: Designs the electronics inside the black boxes.

172

QUALIFICATIONS: Bachelor's or master's degree in electrical engineering. Positions available in full range of experience levels.

JOB TITLE: **Flight Control Design Engineer**

JOB DESCRIPTION: Designs systems electronics for flight controls.

QUALIFICATIONS: Bachelor's or master's degree in electrical engineering plus at least five years' experience.

JOB TITLE: **CRT Design Engineer**

JOB DESCRIPTION: Designs CRT display units used in cockpits in connection with flight control systems.

QUALIFICATIONS: Bachelor's or master's degree in electrical engineering plus at least five years' experience.

JOB TITLE: **Quality Engineer**

JOB DESCRIPTION: Determines methods as well as testing and inspecting programs for manufacturing products to meet military specifications.

QUALIFICATIONS: Bachelor's in electrcal engineering with five years' experience working with military specs.

JOB TITLE: **Standards Engineer**

JOB DESCRIPTION: Works as an in-house specialist and purchasing information resource for buying technical parts.

QUALIFICATIONS: Bachelor's degree in electrical engineering plus five years' experience.

JOB TITLE: **Reliability Engineer**

JOB DESCRIPTION: Determines theoretical failure rate of computer based on computing known failure rates of individual components.

QUALIFICATIONS: Bachelor's degree in electrical engineering plus five years' experience:.

JOB TITLE: **Software Engineer**

JOB DESCRIPTION: Develops software (real-time programming) that operates a system of black boxes.

QUALIFICATIONS: Bachelor's degree in electrical engineering. All levels of experience needed.

Job Title: **Manufacturing Engineer**

JOB DESCRIPTION: Creates process for manufacturing. Brings product from prototype stage to full manufacturing. Devises routing sheets used by assemblers.

QUALIFICATIONS: Bachelor's degree in electrical or industrial engineering or manufacturing technology. All levels of experience needed.

JOB TITLE: **Electronics Technician**

JOB DESCRIPTION: Applies basic electronics technology to one of the following areas: testing products; working in research and development as engineering development technician; programming software for computerized testing equipment; repairing testing equipment.

QUALIFICATIONS: Two-year associate's degree in electronics or equivalent experience. All levels of experience hired.

JOB TITLE: **Assembler**

JOB DESCRIPTION: Places components and performs soldering and wiring assembly tasks.

QUALIFICATIONS: Usually some electronic assembly experience required.

NORTH CAROLINA

The long range goal of the Research Triangle Park in North Carolina is to diversify the state's economic base by attracting high-technology industry.

There's nothing so unusual about that statement until you realize it was made some twenty-five years ago, about the time the park was opened. Longevity has played a major part in making the highly touted Research Triangle Park a front runner today in attracting high-tech companies.

But the other key to success, according to executive director Ned Huffman, is that the park targets companies and carefully limits who sets up shop there. It's a research park. Traditional manufacturing isn't allowed. There's no housing in the park either.

Research Triangle Park grew out of a long history of exchange among three universities—Duke University in Durham, the University of North Carolina in Chapel Hill, and North Carolina State University in Raleigh. They make up points of a triangle, and the area was long referred to informally as the golden triangle.

Today the park seems as serene as it must have when it was a simple forest. The companies that employ thousands there have made certain their buildings blend into the quiet surroundings. Long pine tree-lined drives wind back from the roads to building entrances. The original plan for the 5,500-acre park calls for some 85 percent of the land to be left open.

The area also boasts the largest number of Ph.D. engineers and scientists per 100,000 people in the country.

They live in the surrounding towns, with rolling hills and spacious yards. Mostly engineers from the park built the suburban town of Cary from 5,000 to 25,000 in the last twenty years.

The park has also stimulated tremendous high-tech growth in the surrounding counties—particularly around Raleigh where a host of manufacturing companies employ tens of thousands.

Burroughs Wellcome Co.
Research Triangle Park

COMPANY PROFILE: A unicorn, the mythological symbol of quality and purity, is the fitting corporate emblem for this prestigious pharmaceutical company. Burroughs Wellcome was founded in 1880 in London by two American pharmacists—Silas M. Burroughs and Henry S. Wellcome. In 1906, a U.S. branch was established in New York, and in 1970, the U.S. headquarters and extensive research laboratories were moved to Research Triangle Park. The company is a wholly owned subsidiary of The Wellcome Foundation, a unique philanthropic organization whose only stockholder is The Wellcome Trust. All profits are dispersed throughout the world in support of research in human and veterinary medicine. Over the years, Burroughs Wellcome has been known for its medical support of world explorations. More recently, astronauts took three Burroughs Wellcome products on their journey to the moon. Current research projects include antiviral chemotherapy, a novel antidepressant, a muscle relaxant for use in surgical procedures, and a study of uses of interferon. Today, the facility at Research Triangle Park is the building most often used to represent the park in brochures. It is a multi-layered building of "space-age" design which houses 200 laboratories, a 46,000-volume library, 200-seat auditorium, cafeteria, and corporate offices.

HOW TO APPLY: Send resume to:

> Personnel Department
> Burroughs Wellcome Co.
> 3030 Cornwallis Road
> Research Triangle Park, NC 27709

HOW TO FOLLOW UP: If you send a resume, Burroughs Wellcome will respond with a letter including an application and a brochure about the company. You can return that application, and it will be kept on file for six months. Burroughs Wellcome prefers that you write rather than call concerning the status of your resume.

HOW TO GET THERE: Walk-in applications are taken only on Tuesday between 9 A.M. and 3 P.M. Typing tests are given during these hours only, unless by special appointment. Every Tuesday a list of current job openings is updated and posted in the lobby. Burroughs Wellcome is located about five miles west of the Raleigh-Durham Airport. Take Interstate 40 to Research Triangle Park. Take the Cornwallis Road exit, turn right, and you'll see the Burroughs Wellcome Co. entrance on your left.

PROSPECTS: In mid-1983, the company had more than 1,000 employees at Research Triangle Park and was expecting some growth.

REWARDS: Benefits include tuition reimbursement for approved studies; health, dental, accident, life, and disability insurance plans; retirement plan; optional investment savings plan; discounts on nonprescription items; and periodic physical examinations. Minimum starting pay for professional research lab jobs (with bachelor's or master's degrees) is $1,300 monthly. For most clerical jobs, the minimum to start is $780 monthly.

JOB TITLE: **Research Assistant, Research Scientist**

JOB DESCRIPTION: Jobs most frequently open are in the research laboratories, but they are very specific in nature—from qualifications to job duties—depending on the area of scientific research. Most come under the title of research assistant or research scientist but cover a wide range of credentials and salary levels.

QUALIFICATIONS: Most require bachelor's or master's degrees in chemical/ biological sciences (organic chemistry, chemistry, biochemistry, microbiology, biology, medical technology) and at least a year of experience in the specific area of the opening. There are few openings for Ph.D.'s.

JOB TITLE: **Secretary**

JOB DESCRIPTION: Again, this is a general area of openings which includes a variety of secretaries and clerks.

QUALIFICATIONS: Need at least a year's experience, and Burroughs Wellcome perfers that it be in a similar setting to the job opening. For example, you need knowledge of medical terminology and experience working in a medical environment for some openings. Clerical positions normally require typing speed of 35 correct words per minute.

Data General Corporation

Clayton

COMPANY PROFILE: This Data General facility manufactures the company's general purpose computers. It opened in 1978 and in mid-1983 employed some 800 people.

HOW TO APPLY: Send resume or application to:

Industrial Relations
Data General
P.O. Box 186
Clayton, NC 27520

HOW TO FOLLOW UP: Data General does send a card to acknowledge receipt of your resume. Your application is kept on file for ninety days, and you're contacted if the company wants an interview. You can call a main number, (919) 553-5076, and ask for Employment to learn the status of your application. (Wait at least a couple weeks after you send it.)

HOW TO GET THERE: Data General prefers no walk-in applications.

PROSPECTS: This manufacturing facility reported a strong hiring mode beginning in mid-1983 and anticipated to continue through 1984.

REWARDS: Same as Data General employees corporate-wide. See the Data General listing for Boston, page 164.

JOB TITLE: **Manufacturing Engineer**

JOB DESCRIPTION: Monitors and troubleshoots the manufacturing process. May go back to design team to alter basic product feature for improved manufacturing.

QUALIFICATIONS: Bachelor's degree in industrial, mechanical, or chemical engineering.

JOB TITLE: **Quality Engineer**

JOB DESCRIPTION: Analyzes and troubleshoots production problems in the manufacturing stage. Develops testing procedures to improve product reliability.

QUALIFICATIONS: Bachelor's degree in electrical, chemical, or mechanical engineering plus experience preferred.

JOB TITLE: **Test Engineer**

JOB DESCRIPTION: Designs product testing procedures.

QUALIFICATIONS: Bachelor's degree in electrical engineering.

JOB TITLE: **Technician**

JOB DESCRIPTION: Performs a variety of testing and engineering aide tasks.

QUALIFICATIONS: Two-year associate's degree in electronics.

JOB TITLE: **Electronic Assembler**

JOB DESCRIPTION: Performs a variety of assembly tasks, some using automated equipment.

QUALIFICATIONS: High school diploma plus experience preferred.

Data General Corporation

Research Triangle Park

COMPANY PROFILE: This is Data General's only other facility outside of Westboro, Massachusetts, which is totally devoted to research and development (R&D). Researchers do long-term product strategy research for the corporation as a whole and some specific product development work, which includes both hardware and software development.

HOW TO APPLY: Send resume to:

> Personnel
> Data General
> 62 Alexander Drive
> Research Triangle Park, NC 27709

HOW TO FOLLOW UP: You'll get an acknowledgment post card in response to your resume and a call for an interview in about three weeks if there's an open job match for your skills. Resumes are kept on file for a year.

HOW TO GET THERE: You can drop off your resume in person, but there are no unscheduled interviews. From the Raleigh-Durham Airport, take Interstate 40 west into Research Triangle Park. Exit on Alexander Drive and turn right. Data General is in the second driveway on your right past the first light.

PROSPECTS: The R&D facility is in a moderate growth mode doing most of its hiring activity through regional colleges for entry-level positions.

REWARDS: Same as Data General employees corporate-wide. See the listing for Data General in Boston, page 164.

JOB TITLE: **Engineer**

JOB DESCRIPTION: Works in all facets of hardware and software development for new products.

QUALIFICATIONS: Bachelor's, master's, or Ph.D. degree in electrical engineering, computer science, or new combination degree, computer engineering. Data General likes the combination degree which qualifies the graduate for both software and hardware development.

JOB TIP: This Data General facility is strongly supporting a program of co-operative education with regional schools to allow engineering students hands-on experience. In addition, a company spokesman says any graduates who have work related to their studies on their resumes have an edge for a job.

General Electric, Semiconductor Business Division

Research Triangle Park

COMPANY PROFILE: This high-technology division of General Electric designs, produces, and markets semi-custom gate array integrated circuits (ICs) and custom integrated circuits. It's one of a handful of companies that started the state-of-the-art technology in chipmaking about a year and a half ago. The gate array IC allows a chip customer an intermediate step between a relatively inexpensive mass marketed standard chip and a costly custom chip which can take months, even years, to produce. The gate array chip is partially mass produced with the final circuitry customized. It can be designed and produced in about ten weeks. GE claims to have the newest physical facility in the country for this type of production—a $60 million building housing some of the most advanced state-of-the-art equipment.

HOW TO APPLY: Send resume to:

> Staffing Department
> General Electric
> Semiconductor Business Division
> One Micron Drive
> Research Traingle Park, NC 27709

HOW TO FOLLOW UP: GE does respond to all applications and resumes, but it may take a month or six weeks. The response will be either a letter saying there's no present job match or an invitation for a personal interview. You can write to find out the status of your resume.

HOW TO GET THERE: You can drop off your resume in person, but an interview is unlikely since GE receives as many as one hundred resumes a day. From the Raleigh-Durham Airport, take Interstate 40 west into Research Triangle Park to the Cornwallis Road exit. Bear right, or west, on Cornwallis. GE is about a half a mile on your left.

PROSPECTS: GE moved into its Research Triangle Park facility in March of 1982 and about a year later had some 190 people. The company is in an aggressive growth mode, scheduled to reach 250 total employees by the end of 1983 and add at least another 50 in 1984. Original plans called for some 500 employees by 1985 and from 800 to 1,000 by the 1990s, but new technologies could escalate those projections. Even though GE does some manufacturing, it's such a hybrid manufacturing that people needed are highly skilled. The company is predominantly made up of electronics engineers and computer scientists. Better than 10 percent of the total employees have Ph.D.'s. As of mid-1983, however, the company had many key people in place and was beginning to consider more entry-level engineers and technicians with academic credentials but little or no experience.

REWARDS: A comprehensive GE benefits package and state-of-the-art equipment and development technology make this company an exciting and rewarding place to work.

JOB TITLE: **Advanced Process Development Engineer**

JOB DESCRIPTION: Works to enhance the production process using and developing advanced techniques in wafer fabrication.

QUALIFICATIONS: Bachelor's and master's degrees in electrical engineering for entry level. Higher levels require some experience.

JOB TITLE: **Applications Engineer**

JOB DESCRIPTION: Interfaces between design team and customer to determine what custom or semi-custom IC is needed to fill the customer's needs. Uses computer aided design (CAD) equipment for modeling trial designs.

QUALIFICATIONS: Bachelor's and master's degrees in electronic engineering. Bachelor's alone is good if you designed and processed an IC as a student project.

JOB TITLE: **Test Engineer**

JOB DESCRIPTION: Generates and implements plans for testing prototype products.

QUALIFICATIONS: Bachelor's and master's degrees in electronic engineering.

JOB TITLE: **CMOS Linear Design Engineer**

JOB DESCRIPTION: Designs and develops complementary metal oxide silicon (CMOS) linear circuits.

QUALIFICATIONS: Bachelor's and master's degree in electronic engineering with linear design course work. GE says engineers with this specialty are scarce.

JOB TITLE: **Layout Software Engineer**

JOB DESCRIPTION: Designs software for computer aided design systems used in the design process for CMOS gate array and standard cell ICs.

QUALIFICATIONS: Bachelor's and master's degree in computer science and/or electronic engineering plus experience.

JOB TITLE: **IC Design Engineer**

JOB DESCRIPTION: Designs and develops gate array standard cell and configurable controller ICs, including circuit design, circuit and logic simulation, test generation, chip layout, and design rule checking.

QUALIFICATIONS: Bachelor's and master's degrees in electronic engineering.

JOB TITLE: **Device Implant/Process Control Engineer**

JOB DESCRIPTION: Works with thin film and epi area to set up, sustain, and improve expertise in CMOS production lines.

QUALIFICATIONS: Bachelor's or master's degree in electronic engineering.

JOB TITLE: **CMOS Analog Design Engineer**

JOB DESCRIPTION: Designs OPAMPS, comparators, and switch capacitor circuits.

QUALIFICATIONS: Bachelor's and master's degree in electronic engineering.

JOB TITLE: **IC Layout Designer**

JOB DESCRIPTION: Transforms engineer's design concept into finished drawing using Calma CAD system. Performs testing procedures and brings design drawing to final magnetic tape ready to deliver for use in actual production.

QUALIFICATIONS: Need background in design drafting using CAD system and fundamental knowledge of electronics and math. May have associate's degree in drafting with experience. GE says people for this position are in short supply. Can lead to junior level software designer.

JOB TITLE: **Technician**

JOB DESCRIPTION: Assists engineers in developing and implementing new technologies, assists operators in using precision equipment, maintains equipment to optimum standards. Many technicians specialize in a particular area.

QUALIFICATIONS: Two-year associate's degree in electronics or military training with experience or equivalent experience. GE says it's always looking for good technicians and, like engineers, will hire entry-level positions now.

JOB TIP: General Electric does hire some support and administrative personnel, but usually with very specific qualifications. For instance, in mid-1983, the company was looking for a technical writer who spoke and wrote fluent French.

International Business Machines Corporation (IBM), Communication Products Division

Research Triangle Park

COMPANY PROFILE: IBM's Communication Products Division facilities in Research Triangle Park develop and manufacture communications products including retail and supermarket terminals and subsystems, general purpose terminals, batch and graphic display terminals, distributed processing systems, telecommunications systems, and modems. Advanced communications technologies used include computer interconnection, data base distribution, networking, satellites, analog and digital data processing, and transmission. The site had around 7,000 employees in mid-1983.

HOW TO APPLY: Send resume to:

> IBM Corporation
> Employment Department
> P.O. Box 12195
> Research Triangle Park, NC 27709

HOW TO FOLLOW UP: IBM responds to all applicants by mail. Applicants are asked not to telephone or visit IBM to check on their status.

HOW TO GET THERE: Walk-in applications are accepted but interviews normally are not given at the time of application. Research Triangle Park is located between Raleigh and Durham off Interstate 40, exit 280. Follow signs to IBM.

PROSPECTS: There are limited hiring opportunities. Most professionals are hired off college campuses.

REWARDS: IBM says employee benefits and compensation programs are among the finest in industry. The company uses a merit pay system—advancement based on merit.

JOB TITLE: **Chemical Engineer, Materials Scientist**

JOB DESCRIPTION: Involved in semiconductor processing and module packaging, plastics molding, chemical systems design, process studies, and equipment specifications for holographic devices.

QUALIFICATIONS: Bachelor's, master's, or doctorate degree in chemical engineering or materials science, or equivalent knowledge/experience.

JOB TITLE: **Computer Scientist**

JOB DESCRIPTION: Does system design and architecture; develops and verifies application, diagnostic, communication, and device control programs.

184

QUALIFICATIONS: Bachelor's, master's, or doctorate degree in engineering, computer science, or mathematics or equivalent knowledge/experience.

JOB TITLE: **Electrical Engineer**

JOB DESCRIPTION: Involved in digital and analog logic and circuit design; simulation, microcode development; power systems design; development of test strategies, devices, and systems.

QUALIFICATIONS: Bachelor's, master's, or doctorate degree in electrical engineering or equivalent knowledge/experience.

JOB TITLE: **Industrial Engineer**

JOB DESCRIPTION: Involved in resource planning; design and development of bid proposals for physical facilities for the site.

QUALIFICATIONS: Bachelor's, master's, or doctorate degree in industrial engineering or equivalent knowledge/experience.

JOB TITLE: **Mechanical Engineer**

JOB DESCRIPTION: Involved in packaging design, mechanism design, and implementation; development of test strategies, devices, and systems.

QUALIFICATIONS: Bachelor's, master's, or doctorate degree in mechanical engineering or equivalent knowledge/experience.

JOB TITLE: **Electronics Technician**

JOB DESCRIPTION: Performs analysis, testing, design, and building of electrical, electronic, optical, or electro-mechanical devices, components, and subassemblies.

QUALIFICATIONS: Two-year associate's degree in electronics or equivalent knowledge/experience.

JOB TITLE: **Assembler**

JOB DESCRIPTION: Assembles, adjusts, aligns, and tests part subassemblies and major functional units. Must be able to build from engineering drawings.

QUALIFICATIONS: Various levels of appropriate education and/or experience.

Research Triangle Institute

Research Triangle Park

COMPANY PROFILE: Research Triangle Institute is a not-for-profit corporation affiliated with the three universities—Duke, North Carolina State, and University of North Carolina—which make up the points of Research Triangle Park. The institute, founded with the park in 1959, is the academic research focal point of the area. The institute operates with a regular staff of about 900 (most of whom are research professionals) in fifteen laboratory and office buildings on a 180-acre campus in Research Park. It is self-supporting from research projects contracted by business, industry, governmental bodies, industrial associations, and public service agencies. It sometimes works closely with faculty scientists at the universities on collaborative research programs. The institute's research interests range from social issues and nutritional studies to microelectronics.

The following are among fields of interest and activity at the institute:

Digital systems; toxicology and teratology; alcohol and drug abuse; economics; biomedical engineering; toxic exposure assessment; crime, delinquency, criminal justice; polymers; social program evaluation; drug metabolism; business planning; pharmacology; industrial productivity; process and chemical engineering; environmental sciences; technology transfer; semiconductor devices and systems; corporate development; organic, biorganic, and medicinal chemistry; computer and information sciences; occupational training; alternative energy systems; survey research; product evaluation, marketing; hazardous waste treatment; education; statistical sampling and methodology; particle emissions control; nutrition; microprocessor applications; air navigation; instrumentation and measurement; health systems planning.

HOW TO APPLY: Send resume, academic transcripts, and references to:

> Research Triangle Institute
> Office of Personnel
> P.O. Box 12194
> Research Triangle Park, NC 27709

HOW TO FOLLOW UP: An initial acknowledgment letter is sent upon receipt of applications. Then senior research staff in the appropriate department reviews applicant packages, and a second letter is sent, requesting an interview if there's a job match. You can call the institute's Office of Personnel, (919) 541-6204, to get additional information or check the status of your application.

HOW TO GET THERE: You can apply in person, but not always get an interview. From the Raleigh-Durham Airport, take Interstate 40 west to the Cornwallis Road exit, and turn left. The institute is the first building on the right.

PROSPECTS: Staff needs depend on current contracts.

REWARDS: Salaries are nationally competitive. Benefits are designed for long-term protection for staff and their families. They include life, disability, and medical care insurance; liberal vacation and sick leave; an institute-funded retirement plan; and a tuition reimbursement continuing education program.

JOB TITLE: **Research Science Staff**

JOB DESCRIPTION: Staff researchers operate at various levels according to academic achievement and experience in the following disciplines: chemistry, biology, computer science, toxicology, genetics, economics, political science, psychology, environmental engineering, sociology, statistics, electrical engineering, chemical engineering, management, operations research, and education.

QUALIFICATIONS: Some two-thirds of the professional staff members have postgraduate degrees. Generally, people with bachelor's degrees should apply only with extensive experience.

JOB TITLE: **Technician**

JOB DESCRIPTION: Technicians with a wide range of specialized titles from laboratory, electronics, animal care assistant to maintenance, work as part of the support staff in research laboratories.

QUALIFICATIONS: High school diploma plus two-year associate's degree in specific technology or equivalent experience.

JOB TITLE: **Administrative Careers**

JOB DESCRIPTION: Occasionally, Research Triangle Institute has openings in the following support areas: personnel, purchasing, safety, contract administration, accounting, public information, data services, word processing, security, and maintenance.

QUALIFICATIONS: Academics or experience appropriate to the specific position plus a strong aptitude for dealing with highly technical activities.

TEXAS

Some say Texas was discovered right after air conditioning.

If that wasn't the case, whoever was there before should have waited. Texas is hot—real hot—about six months of the year. It's particularly hot and humid in Dallas and Houston.

Nonetheless, high tech is moving in all over Texas. Austin and San Antonio seem to be the fastest growing Texas high-tech centers. But northwest Dallas and some parts of Houston are getting a fair share as well.

In Dallas, the new high-tech settlement is springing up in northwest Dallas County around the towns of Richardson and Carrollton—pleasant suburban areas with a clean-cut New West style. Dallas is getting its share of the new electronics firms, like Apple and Mostek. And, as home to Texas Instruments, it also has roots in early postwar high-tech development.

Houston has scattered high-tech development. One of the attractions is NASA, which has drawn some of the aerospace support facilities.

There's also an experimental high-tech community which seems to be working called the Woodlands. Mitchell Energy and Development Corporation opened the planned community in 1974. In mid-1983, there were 16,500 residents and some 5,500 jobs. When built out in the year 2010, it's anticipated to have a job base of 100,000.

Because the community wants clean, long-term, successful industry, developers are going after high tech.

Some 1,700 acres in the Woodlands is set aside as Research Forest—to be patterned after Research Triangle Park in North Carolina. Houston Area Research Center (HARC) opened in 1983 in Research Forest as a joint partnership research facility formed by three Texas universities—Rice, University of Houston System, and Texas A & M.

The Texas Medical Center and the University of Houston will also have facilities in Research Forest along with research and development companies from the private sector.

There is high-tech development in both Dallas and Houston but because of their diverse industrial base (and their notoriety as Western energy capitals) they seem less like the prototype new high-tech boom towns.

Apple Computer, Inc.
Dallas

COMPANY PROFILE: Other than California, the north Dallas suburb of Carrollton is the major domestic site for manufacturing Apple computers. By the end of 1983, the Carrollton facility is adding a major printed circuit board operation which will add components to blank boards by a highly automated process. Thus, Apple in Texas is "aggressively moving toward (people) needs in automation, mechanization, and robotics."

HOW TO APPLY: Send resume or write for more information about current openings to:

> Apple Computer, Inc.
> 2724 Realty Road
> 115014
> Carrollton, TX 75011
> Attn: Employment

HOW TO FOLLOW UP: Apple responds to applicants in writing or by phone within a couple of weeks of receiving your resume. You can call a main number, (214) 323-5300, to be certain your material got there. Applications are kept on file for a year.

HOW TO GET THERE: Apple Computer is located on the northwestern intersection of Belt Line Road and Marsh Lane in Carrollton, Texas. It's about twenty miles north of downtown Dallas and about eighteen miles northeast of Dallas-Fort Worth Airport. Heading east on Interstate 635, you take the Marsh Lane exit, turn left on Marsh Lane, and go about five miles. Apple does take walk-in applications in the main lobby reception area, but cannot guarantee an interview on the spot.

PROSPECTS: Apple opened its Texas facility in 1980, had 550 employees in the summer of 1983, and plans on growing to about 750 total employees in 1984. In mid-1983, the company reported at least 100 openings.

REWARDS: Apple bases salary offers on very individualized reviews of an applicant's background and abilities.

JOB TITLE: **Test Engineer A**

JOB DESCRIPTION: Designs, develops, and implements cost-effective methods of testing and troubleshooting systems and equipment. Prepares test and diagnostic programs, designs test fixtures and equipment, completes test specifications and procedures for new products.

QUALIFICATIONS: Bachelor's degree in electrical or electronic engineering or equivalent with five to eight years of related experience.

JOB TITLE: **Electronics Technician**

JOB DESCRIPTION: Assists in establishing electrical test systems.

QUALIFICATIONS: Associate's degree in electronics with two to three years' experience.

JOB TITLE: **Production Engineer A**

JOB DESCRIPTION: Oversees production methods to ensure product standards and profitability and develops and implements plans to bring new products from prototype stage into production.

QUALIFICATIONS: Bachelor's degree in electrical or manufacturing engineering or equivalent with five years' experience in production engineering or related manufacturing activity.

JOB TITLE: **Production Engineering Technician**

JOB DESCRIPTION: Lays out assembly lines, identifies work stations and activities there, documents procedural steps, and improves process flow of work.

QUALIFICATIONS: Two-year vocational course for production technicians and two to three years' experience.

JOB TITLE: **Materials/Quality Assurance Engineer**

JOB DESCRIPTION: Develops, applies, revises, and maintains quality standards for processing materials into partially finished or finished products. Selects materials based on reliability and usability weighed against quality standards.

QUALIFICATIONS: Bachelor's degree in mechanical, electrical, or quality engineering or equivalent with five to eight years' experience in product planning with knowledge of inspection methods in the design, fabrication, and production of electronic components or material and/or electro-mechanical equipment.

JOB TITLE: **Buyer**

JOB DESCRIPTION: Selects best materials or components of electronics products, including everything from blank circuit boards to integrated circuits with quality and pricing as guidelines.

QUALIFICATIONS: Two years' experience in buying electronics materials for lowest level positions (there are several levels of buyers).

JOB TITLE: **Inventory Control/Production/Material Specialist**

JOB DESCRIPTION: Makes sure that the right materials are at the right place at the right time in the manufacturing process. Implements new-style ways of manufacturing like just-in-time inventory.

QUALIFICATIONS: Three to five years' experience in production, sometimes has bachelor's degree in business. Apple says it's particularly looking for specialists in this area from auto companies which have had success with similar production techniques.

JOB TITLE: **Automation/Mechanization Engineer**

JOB DESCRIPTION: Sets up, monitors, installs, and generally oversees automated and robotized systems used for various stages of production.

QUALIFICATIONS: Bachelor's degree in automation or robotics.

JOB TITLE: **Robotics Technician**

JOB DESCRIPTION: Assists the automation/mechanization engineer and maintains and repairs automated systems.

QUALIFICATIONS: Associate's degree in robotics technician or manufacturing engineering technician with robotics experience.

JOB TITLE: **Assembler**

JOB DESCRIPTION: Puts parts together mechanically and performs some electrical tests.

QUALIFICATIONS: Prior electronic assembler experience preferred. This job is being automated to a great degree at Apple, but some assemblers will still be needed to monitor and operate automated processes.

International Business Machines Corporation (IBM), Federal Systems Division

Houston

COMPANY PROFILE: The IBM Federal Systems Division in Houston designs, develops, integrates, tests, and provides operational support of spaceborne and ground-based systems for the government's manned spaceflight program. It had around 700 employees in mid-1983. Products include information processing software and support of space transportation systems, complex data processing and information handling systems for manned space-flight mission planning, real-time mission support, payload data processing, and spaceborne software for manned spacecraft flight control.

HOW TO APPLY: Send resume to:

> IBM—Federal Systems Division
> Employment Department
> 1322 Space Park Drive
> Houston, TX 77058

HOW TO FOLLOW UP: IBM responds to all applicants by mail. Applicants are asked not to telephone or visit IBM to check on their status.

HOW TO GET THERE: Walk-in applications are accepted, but interviews normally are not given at the time of application. From Interstate 45, southeast of Houston, take NASA Road 1 to Nassau Bay Drive (at Holiday Inn); turn right and go one block to Space Park Drive; turn left; the IBM plant is a block away on the right.

PROSPECTS: There are limited hiring opportunities. Most professionals are hired off college campuses.

REWARDS: Employee benefits and compensation programs are among the finest in industry, according to IBM. The company uses a merit pay system—advancement based on performance.

JOB TITLE: **Computer Scientist**

JOB DESCRIPTION: Programs in high order languages on real-time computer system for space applications.

QUALIFICATIONS: Bachelor's, master's, or doctorate degree in engineering, computer science, or mathematics or equivalent knowledge/experience.

JOB TITLE: **Systems Engineer**

JOB DESCRIPTION: Develops architecture for command and control or communications systems.

QUALIFICATIONS: Bachelor's, master's, or doctorate degree in engineering, computer science, or mathematics or equivalent knowledge/experience.

JOB TITLE: **Mathematician, Statistician, Physicist**

JOB DESCRIPTION: Uses computer simulation to analyze spacecraft trajectory, guidance, navigation, and flight control systems.

QUALIFICATIONS: Bachelor's, master's, or doctorate degree in engineering, computer science, mathematics, or physics or equivalent knowledge/experience.

JOB TITLE: **Mechanical Engineer**

JOB DESCRIPTION: Determines spacecraft electronics, structural and installation requirements.

QUALIFICATIONS: Bachelor's, master's, or doctorate degree in aeronautical engineering or mechanical engineering with courses in aeronautical engineering or equivalent knowledge/experience.

Mostek Corporation

Dallas

COMPANY PROFILE: Mostek Corporation is a subsidiary of United Technologies Corporation. The company designs, manufactures, and markets semiconductor devices, MOS (metal oxide silicon) integrated circuits, MOS memory chips, microprocessors and microcomputers, telecommunications circuits, semi-custom integrated circuits, and electronic subsystems. The company, located in one of Dallas' popular suburbs for high-tech development, had more than 4,000 employees in mid-1983.

HOW TO APPLY: Send resume or application to:

> Employment Office
> Mostek Corporation
> 1215 W. Crosby Road
> Carrollton, TX 75006

HOW TO FOLLOW UP: Because of the high volume of applications received, Mostek cannot acknowledge every one. You'll be notified only if the company wants an interview.

HOW TO GET THERE: Mostek does accept walk-in applications, but gives no interviews on the spot. Take Interstate 35 north from Dallas. It will change to Interstate 35 West. Continue to the Valwood Parkway exit. Go west (left) to Monetary Drive. Turn right and then left on Electronics Lane. The Mostek employment office is at 1100 Electronics Lane.

PROSPECTS: Despite layoffs in 1982 because of the depressed economy, Mostek had recalled workers by mid-1983 and was forecasting a continued hiring mode through 1984. The company hires professionals at all levels from entry level to highly experienced. There are some openings for technicians and operators to work in fabrication and test areas.

REWARDS: Mostek offers a highly challenging, competitive, state-of-the-art environment. It has competitive salaries and benefits including medical, dental, and life insurance and a tuition reimbursement plan.

JOB TITLE: **Product Engineer**

JOB DESCRIPTION: Responsible for cost analysis and yield improvement from the wafer fabrication stage to the final shipped unit. Works in all areas from fabrication to testing to assembly and in quality and planning departments.

QUALIFICATIONS: Bachelor's or master's degree in electrical engineering or computer science.

Job Title: **Design Engineer**

JOB DESCRIPTION: Works on either components or systems to create final product design based on concepts and specifications.

QUALIFICATIONS: Bachelor's, master's, or Ph.D. in electrical engineering or master's or Ph.D. in physics plus good background in digital and analog circuit design, MOS device physics, digital systems integration, or computer architecture.

JOB TITLE: **Systems Engineer**

JOB DESCRIPTION: Develops one or more of the following from concept to testing: applications software, development software, diagnostics for micro-processor-based system.

QUALIFICATIONS: Bachelor's or master's degree in electrical engineering or computer science.

JOB TITLE: **Facilities Engineer**

JOB DESCRIPTION: Evaluates needs and costs, directs design, construction, and start-up of an assigned physical plant project.

QUALIFICATIONS: Bachelor's in electrical, chemical, or mechanical engineering.

JOB TITLE: **Test Engineer**

JOB DESCRIPTION: Responsible for testing all Mostek products to be certain they meet specifications with an emphasis on cost effectiveness, test methods, and zero defects.

QUALIFICATIONS: Bachelor's or master's degree in electrical engineering or computer science.

JOB TITLE: **Business Systems Programmer**

JOB DESCRIPTION: Plans and designs corporate business application systems. Job includes developing flow charts, data record formats, and controls as well as writing and testing programs.

QUALIFICATIONS: Bachelor's degree in computer science and/or master's degree in computer science or business administration.

JOB TITLE: **Marketing Area**

JOB DESCRIPTION: Professionals in this area set pricing policies, do strategic planning, and direct promotional policies.

QUALIFICATIONS: Bachelor's degree in electrical engineering, master's in business administration preferred. Need good interpersonal skills to work in fast-paced environment.

JOB TITLE: **Finance Area**

JOB DESCRIPTION: Professionals in this area are responsible for corporate forecasting, managing, and controlling corporate financial functions.

QUALIFICATIONS: Master's in business administration.

JOB TITLE: **Accounting Area**

JOB DESCRIPTION: Professionals perform a wide range of accounting duties, including general ledger, accounts payable, accounts receivable, and payroll accounting.

QUALIFICATIONS: Bachelor's or master's in business administration.

JOB TITLE: **Production Planner**

JOB DESCRIPTION: Plans product line by analyzing profit and capacity, does production scheduling, coordinates manufacturing, and basically manages a production program. Uses computer modeling.

QUALIFICATIONS: Bachelor's or master's in business administration.

JOB TITLE: **Purchasing Area**

JOB DESCRIPTION: Professionals in this area interface with engineers and suppliers to acquire high volume raw materials for semiconductors and electronics.

QUALIFICATIONS: Bachelor's or master's in business administration plus technical degree in electrical, mechanical, industrial, or chemical engineering preferred. Need strong organizing and communications skills.

JOB TITLE: **Production Supervisor**

JOB DESCRIPTION: Directs chemical and physical processes in fabrication area. This is a hands-on position which requires outstanding interpersonal and leadership skills along with technical knowledge.

QUALIFICATIONS: Bachelor's degree in physics, chemistry, general science, or business administration.

Texas Instruments, Inc.

Dallas

COMPANY PROFILE: Texas Instruments (TI) is a multinational company with manufacturing plants in eighteen countries employing some 80,000 people. The great majority of facilities in the U.S. are in Texas. The company was founded in 1930 and is still a leader in electronic technology today. Dallas is the world headquarters for Texas Instruments and its subsidiary, Geophysical Service Inc. TI's Central Research Laboratories are also on the main campus of TI in north Dallas. TI's Dallas manufacturing facility produces semiconductor materials, designs and manufactures transistors, integrated circuits, electronic components, and government electronic systems including radar, infrared, and digital processing equipment.

HOW TO APPLY: You can apply for professional positions at any TI facilities by sending a resume to:

> Texas Instruments Incorporated
> Corporate Staffing
> P.O. Box 225474, M/S 67
> Dallas, TX 75265

Or, you can direct resumes and applications for any positions to the following separate TI divisions in the Dallas area:

> Texas Instruments
> Equipment Group
> P.O. Box 226015, M/S 3186
> Dallas, TX 75266

> TI Information Systems and Services
> P.O. Box 225621, M/S 3609
> Dallas, TX 75266

> Texas Instruments
> Semiconductor Group
> P.O. Box 225012, M/S 11
> Dallas, TX 75265

> Geophysical Service Inc.
> P.O. Box 225621, M/S 3948
> Dallas, TX 75265

TI also has facilities which manufacture everything from semiconductors to personal computers to electronic equipment in Attleboro, Massachusetts; Austin, Texas; Colorado Springs, Colorado; and Houston, Texas, among other locations.

HOW TO FOLLOW UP: All applications for professional positions are acknowledged if sent to the main Corporate Staffing address. Policies differ from one division to another. If you haven't heard anything, TI requests you write instead of call.

HOW TO GET THERE: You can walk in to apply at the main facility in Dallas. From downtown Dallas, take the Central Expressway (Interstate 75) north to Exit 22. You'll see the 500-acre Texas Instruments campus when you exit. Follow signs for the Employment Center.

PROSPECTS: Texas Instruments says it's in an ongoing hiring mode for technical people, but there's little activity for production workers. About 60 percent to 70 percent of the new hires every year are entry-level college graduates. In a good year, TI hires some 2,000 people from the college campus and another 500 to 750 experienced professionals. TI facilities cover the gamut of technologies and technical personnel needs. But most fall into the categories listed below.

REWARDS: In addition to competitive salaries, TI offers a benefits package called Success Sharing in which qualified career TI employees are eligible for profit sharing and retirement plans. TI emphasizes its encouragement of your career potential. Among internal programs is an elaborate job opportunity system in which open positions at all TI locations are circulated among existing employees first. TI has a gym and track on its Dallas site plus a 300-acre recreational area for employees outside Dallas. The Texas Association is an employee recreation group which TI says may be the largest company-sponsored athletic association in the country. Jobs are challenging in state-of-the-art technologies, says TI.

JOB TITLE: **Electronic Engineer**

JOB DESCRIPTION: Works in design functions for a full range of TI products and components.

QUALIFICATIONS: Bachelor's, master's, or Ph.D. in electrical engineering— entry level and experienced.

JOB TITLE: **Computer Scientist**

JOB DESCRIPTION: Develops software for a myriad of application and operating systems.

QUALIFICATIONS: Bachelor's, master's, or Ph.D. in computer science—entry level and experienced.

JOB TITLE: **Mechanical Engineer**

JOB DESCRIPTION: Designs hardware, using a variety of specialty technologies.

QUALIFICATIONS: Bachelor's, master's, or Ph.D. in mechnical engineering— entry level to experienced.

198

JOB TITLE: **Electronic Technician**

JOB DESCRIPTION: Performs testing, troubleshooting, and a full range of technician duties.

QUALIFICATIONS: Two-year associate's degree in technology or comparable military training and experience. Full range of positions available.

AUSTIN

Given a choice, most Texans would prefer to live in Austin, says John Gray, who recruits new high-tech business to the central Texas town.

It's a town unique in Texas—lots of water, attractive hills and green trees, sunny the year around with clean, unpolluted lakes. The city life-style is sophisticated. Cultural activities abound. And Gray says the restaurants rival those in Dallas.

Besides the quality of life, one of the biggest drawing cards for high-tech companies is the University of Texas, the fourth largest university in the nation with graduate programs in engineering, computer science, and business that university officials claim rank in the top 10 percent academically.

A lot of people who go to Austin to school end up staying. So, it's no surprise that a lot of Ph.D.'s drive taxis in Austin.

In 1965, Austin's city fathers launched an economic development program to create jobs for those who wanted to stay there after school and also to improve the city's tax base. With the state capital and the university there, some 50 percent of Austin's land was state-owned and untaxable.

It started working when companies like IBM came to town. Over the years IBM has been followed by Texas Instruments, Motorola, Data General, ROLM, Tandem Computers, and recently, Lockheed Missiles and Space which announced a new facility scheduled to ultimately employ 6,000—mostly engineers.

All in all as of 1983, Austin's economic development campaign aimed at high-tech industry had created 30,000 new manufacturing jobs and 90,000 support and service jobs since it was started seventeen years before. And the momentum was still going.

Advanced Micro Devices, Inc. (AMD)

Austin

COMPANY PROFILE: This facility opened in 1979 for the manufacture and related engineering of AMD's MOS (metal oxide silicon) semiconductors. In the last half of 1983, company headquarters for the Information Products Division and an accompanying test center were being moved to Austin from California. The AMD manufacturing area is looking mostly for production employees, and the new information division needs marketing, finance, and (later in 1984) design personnel. The information division is involved with microprocessors and telecommunication products.

HOW TO APPLY: For AMD manufacturing jobs, send resume to:

> Personnel
> Advanced Micro Devices
> 5204 E. Ben White Blvd.
> Austin, TX 78741

For the Information Products Division, send to:

> Human Resources
> Information Products Division
> Advanced Micro Devices
> 4115 Freidrich Lane
> Austin, TX 78744

HOW TO FOLLOW UP: If you haven't heard from the company in several weeks, you can call for the status of your resume. Call (512) 385-8542 and ask for Personnel for manufacturing and (512) 441-6900 and ask for Human Resources for information products jobs.

HOW TO GET THERE: You can drop off applications or resumes for either facility with the guard at the manufacturing plant. From downtown Austin, take Interstate 35 south to the Ben White exit. Go east (left) about two miles, and you'll see AMD on your left.

PROSPECTS: AMD in Austin is in an aggressive growth mode in keeping with the corporate rate of growth. In particular, the Information Products Division, which had less than 100 people in mid-1983, was expected to reach some 500 employees in 1984.

REWARDS: AMD in Austin has salaries, benefits, and a corporate lifestyle in keeping with corporate-wide standards. See the listing for AMD in California, page 91.

MANUFACTURING JOBS

Job titles hired for on an ongoing basis in Austin are similar to those in AMD in San Antonio except Austin works with MOS technology and San Antonio, bipolar.

INFORMATION PRODUCTS DIVISION JOBS

JOB TITLE: **Product Marketing Manager**

JOB DESCRIPTION: Manages a product line including interfacing with customers and design and manufacturing engineer. Also does strategic planning.

QUALIFICATIONS: Bachelor's in electrical engineering and master's in business administration with experience in the telecommunications market.

JOB TITLE: **Product Marketing Engineer**

JOB DESCRIPTION: Performs technical hands-on work with both microprocessor and telecommunications products.

QUALIFICATIONS: Bachelor's degree in electrical engineering plus one to three years' experience.

JOB TITLE: **Product Line Analyst**

JOB DESCRIPTION: Does financial forecasting, strategic planning for a product line.

QUALIFICATIONS: Usually master's in business administration and two to three years' high-tech experience.

JOB TITLE: **Electronics Technician**

JOB DESCRIPTION: Tests final products.

QUALIFICATIONS: Two-year associate's degree, experience preferred.

Data General Corporation

Austin

COMPANY PROFILE: This facility designs and manufactures peripherals and had some 350 employees in mid-1983.

HOW TO APPLY: Send resume to:

Data General
2706 Montopolis Drive
Austin, TX 78741
Attn: Employment

HOW TO FOLLOW UP: The company will acknowledge your resume within two weeks. Sometime after that, Data General contacts you if it wants an interview. You can call for more information about your resume status to the main number, (512) 385-9740, ask for Employment.

HOW TO GET THERE: Interviews are by appointment only.

PROSPECTS: Data General's current facility is built to accommodate ultimately some 700 employees. The company says it's aggressively recruiting professionals, but anticipates limited production hiring at least through the end of 1983.

REWARDS: Data General in Austin offers the same perks and benefits as all facilities corporate-wide (see page 164). In addition, the new campus-like facility set on 100 acres atop a hill overlooking the city, is an especially attractive and comfortable work setting.

JOB TITLE: **Design Engineer—Software/Hardware**

JOB DESCRIPTION: Creates either digital logic design or microprocessor-based terminal design.

QUALIFICATIONS: Data General hires a full range of engineers in all disciplines from entry level with only a bachelor's degree (in this case usually electrical engineering or computer science) to advanced degrees with several years' experience. Engineer levels range from Engineer I to Principal Engineer.

JOB TITLE: **Manufacturing Engineer**

JOB DESCRIPTION: Designs and directs all manufacturing processes to gain maximum cost effectiveness and quality production.

QUALIFICATIONS: Full range of positions, usually need industrial or process engineering disciplines.

JOB TITLE: **Programmer**

JOB DESCRIPTION: Designs software (including color and graphics) for Data General products.

QUALIFICATIONS: Full range of positions, usually need electrical engineering or computer science degree.

W.L. Gore & Associates, Inc., Electronics Products Division

Austin

COMPANY PROFILE: Gore & Associates manufactures custom designed wire and cable interconnects made from state-of-the-art material to solve electrical, chemical, mechanical, and dimensional problems.

HOW TO APPLY: Send applications and/or resumes to:

W.L. Gore & Associates
P.O. Drawer Q
Manor, TX 78653

HOW TO FOLLOW UP: If you don't have an application or want to be certain yours was received, you can call (512) 276-7600. Gore responds to all applications with a letter explaining company interviewing procedures in detail.

HOW TO GET THERE: You can apply in person at the company located at 7811 Burleson-Manor Road. If you're coming from Austin, take FM969 (Webberville Road) east to the Burleson-Manor Road turn-off (exactly 9.5 miles after crossing Highway 183). Turn left and go one mile up Burleson-Manor Road to the Gore gate on your right. If you're coming from Manor, take Highway 290 to FM973 and turn left. Go to Blake Manor Road (third turn), turn left and continue for about 4.5 miles to Burleson-Manor Road. Turn right and go two miles to the Gore gate.

PROSPECTS: Gore projects adding about 100 new employees by the end of 1984. In mid-1983, the company employed about 50 people. The bulk of the hiring will be for entry-level production associates.

REWARDS: Gore says it offers better than average benefits and competitive salaries in the Austin area.

JOB TITLE: **Production Associate**

JOB DESCRIPTION: Operates automated machinery in the production of wire and cable interconnects.

QUALIFICATIONS: Basic high school education, preferably with an emphasis on math and science. No experience necessary.

JOB TITLE: **Electrical/Machine Maintenance Technician**

JOB DESCRIPTION: Builds new production machinery and maintains and modifies existing production machinery.

QUALIFICATIONS: Basic high school with trade or vocational-technical training in machine shop, electrical, or electronic courses.

JOB TITLE: **Clerical Support**

JOB DESCRIPTION: Supports manufacturing and sales activities with accountant and secretarial skills. Increasingly uses computerized systems.

QUALIFICATIONS: Business school training and/or experience is preferred.

International Business Machines Corporation (IBM), Communication Products Division

Austin

COMPANY PROFILE: The IBM Communication Products Division in Austin develops and manufactures office systems and intelligent terminals supporting data entry and automated office applications including text processing, word processing, and distributed data processing, as well as printer circuit components and printers for office systems. It had some 6,500 employees in mid-1983.

HOW TO APPLY: Send resume to:

IBM
Employment Department
11400 Burnet Road
Austin, TX 78758

HOW TO FOLLOW UP: IBM responds to all applicants by mail. Applicants are asked not to telephone or visit IBM to check on their status.

HOW TO GET THERE: Walk-in applications are accepted but interviews normally are not given at the time of application. Burnet Road is Texas Route 1325, three miles north of Research Boulevard (U.S. Route 183).

PROSPECTS: There are limited hiring opportunities. Most professionals are hired off college campuses.

REWARDS: Employee benefits and compensation programs are among the finest in industry, according to IBM. The company uses a merit pay system—advancement based on performance.

JOB TITLE: **Electrical Engineer**

JOB DESCRIPTION: Works in logic design, product definition, system design, microprocessor design, and adapters for controllers; digital filters and communications; and analog circuit design.

QUALIFICATIONS: Bachelor's, master's, or doctorate degree in electrical engineering or equivalent knowledge/experience.

JOB TITLE: **Chemical Engineer, Industrial Engineer, Materials Scientist, Metallurgical Engineer, Mechanical Engineer**

JOB DESCRIPTION: Works on chemical processes and materials used in manufacture of office products, including lamination, plating, photolithography, and etching.

QUALIFICATIONS: Bachelor's, master's, or doctorate degree in materials science or chemical, industrial, metallurgical, or mechanical engineering or equivalent knowledge/experience.

JOB TITLE: **Computer Scientist, Mathematician, Physicist**

JOB DESCRIPTION: Works in system design and architecture, software development, communication, and device control programs.

QUALIFICATIONS: Bachelor's, master's, or doctorate degree in computer science, mathematics, or physics or equivalent knowledge/experience.

JOB TITLE: **Electronics Technician**

JOB DESCRIPTION: Performs analysis, testing, design, and building of electrical, electronic, optical, or electro-mechanical devices, components, and subassemblies.

QUALIFICATIONS: Two-year associate's degree in electronics or equivalent knowledge/experience.

JOB TITLE: **Assembler**

JOB DESCRIPTION: Assembles, adjusts, aligns, and tests part subassemblies and major functional units. Must be able to build from engineering drawings.

QUALIFICATIONS: Various levels of appropriate education and/or experience.

ROLM Corporation, Office Systems Division

Austin

COMPANY PROFILE: The Office Systems Division of ROLM opened in Austin in the spring of 1981 and introduced its first product, "Cypress," in the spring of 1983. ROLM develops and manufactures its own product line here. The company plans to move to larger rented facilities this fall and build on land it has already purchased in the next couple of years.

HOW TO APPLY: After October, 1983, send resume or application to:

ROLM Corporation
2420 Ridgepoint Drive
Austin, TX 78754

HOW TO FOLLOW UP: ROLM sends an acknowlegment letter soon after receiving your application. If there's an open position in your job match area, your application or resume is forwarded to the manager in charge of that department who decides whether to call you for an interview. If there's nothing currently open for you, your resume is held on file for the balance of the current year and through the following calendar year. You can call (512) 479-5000, extension 2005, for current job openings.

HOW TO GET THERE: You can drop your resume or application, but not get an interview on the spot. ROLM is located at the junction of Highways 183 and 290.

PROSPECTS: ROLM had about 135 employees in mid-1983 and expected to have more than 200 by sometime in 1984. The company currently is about half research and development and half manufacturing, but plans to be a full scale manufacturing facility in addition to its R&D in the next couple of years. Depending on the success of new product development, the facility is projected to hire as many as 2,000 people in this decade. Current needs are mostly in manufacturing, but occasionally the research and development area may need one or more of the following: software engineer, hardware development engineer, power system development engineer, technical writer, support documentation staff, drafter. ROLM also is accepting applications from electrical engineers with specialties in process engineering, production, and quality assurance, and support staff such as buyers and planners.

REWARDS: Current employees say one of the benefits of working there is the "electricity" generated by the excitement of being in on the ground floor of a growing company developing and building new products. Benefits and salaries are on a par with California, where the company headquarters are located. See pages 116 and 150.

JOB TITLE: **Electronic Assembler**

JOB DESCRIPTION: Assembles the basics of the products from breadboards to mechanical frames and operates wave soldering equipment.

QUALIFICATIONS: Need experience and skill level and commitment to turn out high quality product.

JOB TITLE: **Electronics Technician**

JOB DESCRIPTION: Tests and inspects products in research and development and manufacturing stages. Eventually will need to maintain equipment.

QUALIFICATIONS: Two-year associate's degree or vocational school certification in electronics or equivalent experience. College courses or experience like military training acceptable.

JOB TITLE: **Quality Assurance Engineer/Inspector**

JOB DESCRIPTION: Inspects and tests incoming components and outgoing finished products.

QUALIFICATIONS: Experience most important. May have two-year technical degree or bachelor's in electrical engineering for exempt positions.

SAN ANTONIO

If you've heard anything about San Antonio, you've probably heard about the River Walk. It's the tourist development built on two levels along the San Antonio River which runs through downtown. I spent a late afternoon at a sidewalk cafe there drinking sangria and enjoying the perfect temperature in March.

Tourists floated by on a mile and a half leisurely boat trip down the river while others strolled along the walkway, stopping in shops and restaurants. It was a far cry from the traditional Texas images of sage brush and ten-gallon hats.

Above was downtown San Antonio with its quaint narrow streets. The Alamo was just a block from the River Walk.

Until recently, San Antonio's largest employers were five military bases that hired civilians mostly as airplane mechanics.

But by 1983, San Antonio, especially with the election of the aggressive Mayor Henry Cisneros, had become legitimate competition in the high-tech race.

Highway 410, which loops around the outskirts of the city, is the site of a lot of the high-tech growth.

The prestigious Southwest Research Institute is San Antonio's research base. It was started thirty-five years ago, about the same time as Stanford Research International, associated with Stanford University. Southwest does mostly research contract work for Fortune 500 companies.

Although it's not directly involved in work for many of the new-style high-tech companies, Southwest does create a research atmosphere in the community. Researchers can find other researchers to talk to.

Advanced Micro Devices, Inc. (AMD)

San Antonio

COMPANY PROFILE: Advanced Micro Devices opened a facility in San Antonio in the spring of 1983 for five-inch bipolar wafer fabrication. The facility was state-of-the-art and claimed by AMD to be the most advanced of its type in existence in mid-1983.

HOW TO APPLY: Send resume to:

> Personnel Manager
> Advanced Micro Devices, Inc.
> 8611 Military Drive West
> San Antonio, TX 78245

HOW TO FOLLOW UP: AMD sends an acknowledgment card upon receipt of your resume. That's followed in another two to three weeks by a letter indicating the company's interest in you. If you want more information about your status, the company requests that you write instead of calling.

HOW TO GET THERE: You can walk in to apply, but no interviews are given at that time. From San Antonio International Airport, take Loop 410 west to the frontage road exit just past the Culebra exit. This puts you on Military Drive West. Bear right, and the drive takes you to the front entrance of Advanced Micro Devices.

PROSPECTS: In mid-1983, Advanced Micro Devices had more than 100 employees and anticipated hiring about 100 more by January of 1984. The company is in the first of a three-building campus which when completely occupied in the next ten years could employ some 3,000 people. Company spokesmen describe hiring as aggressive—adding some twenty new employees monthly, about 60 percent in production areas.

REWARDS: Rewards are in keeping with Advanced Micro Devices corporate-wide policies. See the listing for AMD in California, page 91.

JOB TITLE: **Operator**

JOB DESCRIPTION: Performs a variety of tasks in the front-end fabrication area.

QUALIFICATIONS: Full range of hires from inexperienced trainee with a minimum high school diploma to senior operators who bring some years of experience. All need dexterity, attention to detail, and ability to follow written directions.

JOB TITLE: **Line Maintenance Technician**

JOB DESCRIPTION: Troubleshoots and performs preventative maintenance on all production and test equipment.

QUALIFICATIONS: Two-year associate's degree in electronics technology, experience preferred.

JOB TITLE: **Product Engineer**

JOB DESCRIPTION: Evaluates wafer products in order to increase yield enhancement while maintaining and improving product reliability and production flow.

QUALIFICATIONS: Bachelor's or master's degree in electrical engineering, computer science, or solid state physics. Full range of positions open from entry level to five or more years' experience.

JOB TITLE: **Process Sustaining/Process Development Engineer**

JOB DESCRIPTION: Develops advanced processes for the development and production of state-of-the-art integrated circuits using advanced bipolar process technologies, including photoresist, diffusion, dual-layer metalization, and ion implantation.

QUALIFICATIONS: Bachelor's, master's, or Ph.D. in electrical or chemical engineering, solid state physics, materials science, or any physical science. This position requires the largest number of people. Full range of positions open.

JOB TITLE: **Test Engineer**

JOB DESCRIPTION: Selects production testing equipment and writes software for production testing and test operating systems.

QUALIFICATIONS: Bachelor's or master's degree in electrical engineering or computer science. Full range of positions open.

Datapoint Corporation

San Antonio

COMPANY PROFILE: Datapoint Corporation is one of the oldest and largest high-tech companies in San Antonio. The company designs and manufactures computer hardware and software for business markets. The company is headquartered in San Antonio where it operates research and development, manufacturing, marketing, and service facilities. It also has manufacturing facilities in Forth Worth, Texas, and Sunnyvale, California, as well as in Europe, Canada, South America, and the Pacific Basin. The company employs a total of 9,000 people—6,000 of them in the United States and more than 3,000 of those in San Antonio.

HOW TO APPLY: Datapoint requests a detailed resume including educational background, work experience, and salary history be sent to:

> Professional Staffing Department
> Datapoint Corporation
> 9725 Datapoint Drive, MS-G05
> San Antonio, TX 78284

HOW TO FOLLOW UP: All applicants for professional positions receive a written response indicating the current needs in that area. If your qualifications match an opening, a recruiter conducts a phone interview. If there's still mutual interest, the company pays for an interview trip to the appropriate facility. You can call the employment department, (512) 699-7411, to check the status of your resume. Resumes are kept on file for one year.

HOW TO GET THERE: Datapoint does accept walk-in applications from 8 A.M. to 4 P.M. Monday through Friday at the Corporate Employment Office. From San Antonio International Airport, take Loop 410 west to Interstate 10 West. Take the second exit, Wurzbach Road, and turn left. The second intersection is Datapoint Drive. Turn left. The employment office is the first building on the left at the intersection of Datapoint Drive and Wurzbach Road.

PROSPECTS: Datapoint hires a "substantial" number of people in all job categories for entry-level and intermediate positions throughout the year. The company describes the positions listed as being in "high demand" most of the time. Unskilled workers, called line operators, do the basic assembly at Datapoint. They are all hired locally and can advance within the company to special operator and lead operator. Recruiters say they hire several dozen new operators each year, but as of now have plenty of applications on file.

REWARDS: Datapoint has a strong policy of promotion from within. There are defined growth paths into managerial, engineering, and operations as well as technical specialist positions. Most engineering and professional positions start at

$26,000. Technician positions start at $14,000. Financial and marketing position salaries vary with credentials and experience.

JOB TITLE: **Electrical Engineer**

JOB DESCRIPTION: Digital engineers are involved in product definition, design, and testing. Hardware implementations include state-of-the-art high-density bipolar, MOS (metal oxide silicon), and related technologies.
   Analog engineers are involved in product design and/or testing.

QUALIFICATIONS: A bachelor's or master's degree in electrical engineering plus minimum two years' experience.

JOB TITLE: **Test Engineer**

JOB DESCRIPTION: Designs and develops test instrumentation from concept to implementation, writes software for automated test systems, plans test schemes, and researches state-of-the-art testing techniques and equipment. Product line includes microprocessor-based CPUs (central processing units), memory systems, power supplies, analog control circuits, printers, tape drives, and disk assemblies.

QUALIFICATIONS: Bachelor's or master's degree in electrical engineering plus minimum two years' experience.

JOB TITLE: **Industrial/Manufacturing Engineer**

JOB DESCRIPTION: Involved in facility planning, design review of new products, advance manufacturing studies on new products, capital equipment justification, and value engineering studies on current and future products to affect maximum cost reduction and product flow.

QUALIFICATIONS: Bachelor's or master's in industrial engineering plus minimum two years' experience.

JOB TITLE: **Quality Engineer**

JOB DESCRIPTION: Assures that new and existing products meet design specifications by testing, reliability studies, and product audits.

QUALIFICATIONS: Bachelor's or master's degree in engineering plus minimum two years' experience.

JOB TITLE: **Software Design Programmer, Systems Analyst, Systems Support**

JOB DESCRIPTION: Works with new product development, hardware/software analysis, and system configuration trade-offs. Develops firmware, microcode, and diagnostics for microprocessor-based systems. May also work as system/

software programmers in new product development, product enhancements, system strategies, and design. Software products include operating systems, input/output control, communications subsystems, languages, and system utility projects.

QUALIFICATIONS: Bachelor's or master's degree in computer science plus minimum two years' experience.

JOB TITLE: **Technician**

JOB DESCRIPTION: Needs a comprehensive knowledge of electronics including the ability to read and interpret schematics and electrical diagrams. Tests, aligns, troubleshoots, and repairs subassemblies and systems. Also troubleshoots malfunctions at board and/or component level using schematics, logic diagrams, wire lists, and test equipment. (minimal supervision)

QUALIFICATIONS: Associate's degree in electronics from an accredited college. No previous experience required.

JOB TITLE: **CAD Operator**

JOB DESCRIPTION: Generates printed writing board artworks and documentation using the computer aided design (CAD) system.

QUALIFICATIONS: Associate's degree in drafting technology plus three years' experience, particularly with knowledge of printed wiring board documentation.

JOB TITLE: **Auditor, Accountant**

JOB DESCRIPTION: Performs various accounting duties, including specialized positions in tax, cost, SEC reporting, consolidation reporting, and general ledger. International and domestic auditing includes electronic data processing (EDP), operations, and internal audits.

QUALIFICATIONS: Bachelor's degree in business plus minimum two years' experience required for all positions. CPA is preferred for accountants. CPA or CIA plus four years' audit experience in an established public accounting firm is required for auditors.

JOB TITLE: **Financial Analyst**

JOB DESCRIPTION: Responsibilities may include the following: financial modeling, strategic planning, financial reporting, pricing analysis, cash flow analysis, investment analysis, product development projections, direct labor forecasting, material inventory forecasting.

QUALIFICATIONS: Bachelor's degree in business plus either a master's in business administration or two years' experience in an industrial environment.

JOB TITLE: **Instructor**

JOB DESCRIPTION: Organizes and administers training programs for both employees and customers of Datapoint. The instruction ranges from relatively simple training handled by associate instructors to more complex training functions handled by technical instructors, senior instructors, and training specialists.

QUALIFICATIONS: Bachelor's degree in business, computer science, or engineering.

JOB TITLE: **Technical Writer**

JOB DESCRIPTION: Organizes, writes, and edits complex information developed by programmers and engineers into a style that is easily understood. Writes books and manuals for customers and for maintenance and installations specialists.

QUALIFICATIONS: Prefer degree in English, journalism, or computer science.

JOB TITLE: **Product Specialist**

JOB DESCRIPTION: Coordinates planning and marketing for current or proposed products; recommends enhancements to existing products; prepares market analyses on Datapoint and competitor's products; coordinates pre-release and pilot test market activities.

QUALIFICATIONS: Degree in business or computer science plus at least four years' experience in data processing or telecommunications.

JOB TITLE: **Product Planner**

JOB DESCRIPTION: Researches and proposes detailed new product definitions; coordinates modifications, expansion, or redefinition of existing products; recommends specific development and support activities; tracks costs associated with products; initiates and coordinates written material to go with products.

QUALIFICATIONS: Degree in computer science or engineering plus at least three years' experience in product planning, development, support, and marketing.

JOB TITLE: **Systems Engineer**

JOB DESCRIPTION: Provides customers and Datapoint field sales staff with systems analysis and design assistance and software support for product line.

QUALIFICATIONS: Degree in computer science or engineering and at least one year's experience in programming, systems analysis, and design.

JOB TITLE: **Sales Representative**

JOB DESCRIPTION: Maintains contact with existing customers and assists in presentations to potential customers as well as coordinates installation and maintenance of equipment.

QUALIFICATIONS: Bachelor's degree in business administration plus at least two years' sales experience in the computer industry.

JOB TITLE: **Customer Service Engineer**

JOB DESCRIPTION: Diagnoses, installs, maintains, and modifies Datapoint equipment at customer's location. Responsible for high level of customer satisfaction.

QUALIFICATIONS: High school plus two years formal electronic technical training or equivalent. No other experience required.

UTAH

Utah is the fourth fastest growing state in the country. If the borders were sealed, it would still be the eleventh fastest growing state because Utah has the highest national birthrate. The predominance of Mormon culture, which emphasizes the importance of family life and encourages large families, is responsible.

At the same time, people in Utah also are among the most educated in the country. For years, the state lost its most talented children because it could offer them no jobs. In the 1970s, Utah started trying to do something about that—including targeting new high-tech industries to settle there.

The transition to high tech seems to be working. Sperry, which actually has been in Salt Lake City for years, just became the area's largest employer. The company, which makes office processors and micro- and minicomputers, has been growing while the area smokestack mainstays, Kenicott Copper and Geneva Steel, have been declining.

For some time, Salt Lake City has been a leader in biomedical research—but only made national headlines with artificial heart recipient, Barney Clark in 1983. Several medical high-tech companies are located around the Utah Medical Center.

Other high-tech companies, like National Semiconductor and Applied Digital Data, have opened satellite facilities in south Salt Lake City. Signetics is in Provo.

Salt Lake City also landed a big service industry in 1983 when American Express bought fifty-three acres for its travelers check service center. It's projected utlimately to employ 1,200 people in a highly computerized operation.

Economic developers say the biggest problem promoting Salt Lake City is the misconception of Utah as a cloistered environment controlled by the Mormons. It's hard to dispel that image when at the very center of downtown, at the point from which streets are numbered in four directions, sits the Mormon Temple with personal guides on duty.

Drinking is responsible for the other predominant Utah reputation. There's a law against serving liquor by the drink. No real problem though. At the restaurant door you simply purchase your pinch bottles over the counter, then pay $1 or $2 for a set-up inside. There are no bars per se—but there are private residence clubs, and everybody belongs to one or two.

So what does Salt Lake City offer the new-style, young, unconnected $50,000-a-year engineer?

The Chamber of Commerce says: "We can give him housing (just slightly above the national average), country clubs, culture probably better than he came from, recreation like he's never experienced it before, including twice the average number of golf and tennis courts per capita. Within a day's drive of Salt Lake, he's got five national parks. Just thirty minutes from downtown, he can ski, hunt, water ski (Lake Powell), backpack, jeep, and hang glide.''

There's skiing at Alta and Snowbird. The Great Salt Lake just west of the city completes the package—beaches, desert, mountains.

Familiar signs of high-tech growth are evident in Salt Lake City. New housing developments are springing up mostly south of the downtown area—some in the foothills.

And the new commercial industrial parks—the standard warehouse-type units—were standing ready to be occupied. For a time, however, the old wide open spaces prevail. As I pulled out of the new International Center development near sunset, I was indeed surprised to come upon a flock of sheep being herded by a man on horseback down the paved development drive.

Sperry

Salt Lake City

COMPANY PROFILE: Sperry, now Salt Lake City's largest employer with 4,100 people, has a campus of several plants with a nucleus of expertise involved in a wide range of product development, engineering, operations, marketing, product testing, customer services, and communications activities. There are two broad operating groups. The Communications Systems and Terminal Product Division is dedicated to the development, manufacturing, and support needs for all terminals, communications, and small business systems and their operating software within the Salt Lake City operations. The Defense Systems Division, Microwave Data Transmission Systems, is responsible for the development, marketing, and logistical support of telecommunications, tactical command/control, and intelligence systems delivered to the U.S. government.

HOW TO APPLY: Send resume or application to:

Employment Manager
Sperry
322 North 2200 West
Salt Lake City, UT 84116

HOW TO FOLLOW UP: You will receive a letter in response to your resume. If Sperry is interested in you, you'll also receive a telephone call or letter in about three weeks to arrange for a personal interview. Resumes are kept on file for three months. Because of the volume of applications, Sperry cannot offer information about the status of your resume by phone.

HOW TO GET THERE: You can apply in person, but don't expect an interview. From Salt Lake City Airport, go east (toward downtown) two miles. Turn left on 2200 West. Sperry is about a half a mile on your right. Look for signs indicating the employment office.

PROSPECTS: Sperry says it recruits for the positions listed on a continuous basis.

REWARDS: Sperry says its salaries are competitive nationally—for professionals generally in the $20,000 to $40,000 range. Benefits include education tuition reimbursement for advanced technology studies; comprehensive medical/disability, life, dental, and travel insurance programs; a retirement plan; income assistance (including accident and sickness); paid holidays and vacations; a stock purchase plan; matching gifts program; merit scholarships for dependents; and company-sponsored training programs. Recreational activities and events are planned for employees and their families throughout the year.

JOB TITLE: **Diagnostic Engineer**

JOB DESCRIPTION: Develops software for testing and diagnosing micro-processor systems and peripherals.

QUALIFICATIONS: Bachelor's degree in computer science or electrical engineering with Assembly language background and experience.

JOB TITLE: **Programmer**

JOB DESCRIPTION: Assignments include computer terminal and small system development involving personal computing and CP/M language operating systems, graphics and CRT control, communications, input/output control, and LAN and PDN development among other challenges at the forefront of microprocessor system application. (LAN and PDN=languages used to interface computers)

QUALIFICATIONS: Bachelor's degree in computer science or electrical engineering plus at least one year's experience in assembly level Z80 and/or M68000 programming.

JOB TITLE: **Scientific Programmer**

JOB DESCRIPTION: Writes microprocessor programming.

QUALIFICATIONS: Bachelor's degree in electrical engineering or computer science or math plus experience in real-time process control using PDP-11, HP-9845, UYK/20, UYK-44 hardware, and FORTRAN IV, BASIC, CMS-2 languages and/or SDEX 20 operating systems.

JOB TITLE: **Terminal Design Engineer**

JOB DESCRIPTION: Works on the development of new terminal products. Assignments include peripheral interface design, telephonics, communications, graphics, and color terminal design.

QUALIFICATIONS: Bachelor's degree in electrical engineering plus at least three years' logic design experience working with microprocessors and digital circuitry.

JOB TITLE: **Video Design Engineer**

JOB DESCRIPTION: Works in analog and video display design.

QUALIFICATIONS: Bachelor's or master's in electrical engineering plus at least three years' experience with CRT display control electronics, high-voltage power supplies, and CRT deflection circuit design and related aspects.

JOB TITLE: **Peripheral Engineer**

JOB DESCRIPTION: Does design and qualification test of terminal peripnerals.

QUALIFICATIONS: For senior level positions, bachelor's degree in electrical or mechanical engineering plus five years' experience in small peripheral product

222

lines. At least three years' experience should be with emphasis on Winchester disk, flexible disk, or advanced printer technology. Also need directly related experience in recording techniques and head and actuator design. Practical experience in selection and qualification of small peripherals preferred.

JOB TITLE: **Manufacturing Engineer**

JOB DESCRIPTION: Creates and implements the manufacturing plan and processes for taking prototype products into full-scale production.

QUALIFICATIONS: Bachelor's degree in electrical, mechanical, or industrial engineering plus at least four years' design, manufacturing, or industrial engineering experience with newly designed terminals, peripherals, or communications products.

JOB TITLE: **Power Supply Design Engineer**

JOB DESCRIPTION: Designs specialized high-voltage power supplies for airborne and terminal applications.

QUALIFICATIONS: At least bachelor's degree in electrical engineering or equivalent—master's preferred—plus at least four years' experience, including familiarity with packaging and thermal control techniques.

JOB TITLE: **Mechanical Engineer**

JOB DESCRIPTION: Designs electronic packaging for airborne applications and communications terminal products.

QUALIFICATIONS: Bachelor's degree in mechanical engineering or equivalent plus five to seven years' experience.

JOB TITLE: **Field Engineer**

JOB DESCRIPTION: Operates and maintains complex microwave digital data link systems.

QUALIFICATIONS: Bachelor's degree in electrical engineering or equivalent plus three to five years' experience on data links, communications systems, aircraft guidance control systems or related electronic equipment. Requires travel and U.S. citizenship.

JOB TITLE: **RF Systems Design Engineer**

JOB DESCRIPTION: Designs radio frequency (RF) systems and components.

QUALIFICATIONS: Bachelor's degree in electrical engineering—master's preferred—with four to seven years' experience in detailed design of RF systems, components, or spread spectrum communications, error correction techniques, advanced antenna systems, RF systems analysis, and RF miniaturization. U.S. citizenship required.

JOB TITLE: **Signal Process Design Engineer**

JOB DESCRIPTION: Designs and develops airborne hardware using state-of-the-art technologies in both RF and digital.

QUALIFICATIONS: Master's in electrical engineering or physics preferred with at least six years' experience in real-time signal processor design. Must be U.S. citizen.

JOB TITLE: **Communications Systems Engineer**

JOB DESCRIPTION: Responsible for military communications system design and analysis using the principles of digital data transmission, spread spectrum, time/frequency division multiple access, encryption, forward error correction, and data interweaving. Also use basics of satellite communication, wide-band telecommunication, line-of-sight duplex (air to ground), and tropo-scatter systems.

QUALIFICATIONS: Master's or Ph.D. in electrical engineering with minimum of seven years' experience in above technologies. Must be U.S. citizen.

JOB TITLE: **IEW Systems Engineer**

JOB DESCRIPTION: Supplies technical engineering support to marketing efforts.

QUALIFICATIONS: Bachelor's degree in electrical engineering with at least five years' experience in intelligence and electronic warfare (IEW) systems. Need U.S. citizenship.

JOB TITLE: **Digital/Analog Systems Engineer**

JOB DESCRIPTION: Coordinates building and integration of communications systems with the design engineering and manufacturing groups. Participates in systems testing in-house and at field locations.

QUALIFICATIONS: Bachelor's degree in electrical engineering—master's preferred—plus at least five years' experience in digital/analog communications and/or avionics systems.

JOB TITLE: **Voice Technology Engineer**

JOB DESCRIPTION: Develops terminal-based voice synthesis and recognition products.

QUALIFICATIONS: Bachelor's or master's degree in electrical engineering with minimum of three years' experience in telephone interface, PABX design, and voice synthesis.

JOB TITLE: **Industrial Engineer**

JOB DESCRIPTION: Develops and implements more effective and cost efficient methods in manufacturing, materials handling, and packaging.

QUALIFICATIONS: Bachelor's degree in industrial engineering or equivalent with two to five years' experience.

JOB TITLE: **Production Control Specialist**

JOB DESCRIPTION: Plans and implements project schedules, recommends improvements, and sets up controls.

QUALIFICATIONS: Bachelor's degree in industrial management or equivalent plus four years' production control experience in manufacturing environment.

JOB TITLE: **Accountant, Budget Analyst, Cost Analyst**

JOB DESCRIPTION: Prepares budgets, financial plans, accounting records, and statistical analyses.

QUALIFICATIONS: Bachelor's degree in business administration or accounting/finance.

JOB TITLE: **Technician**

JOB DESCRIPTION: Designs, constructs, troubleshoots, repairs, calibrates, and operates special electronic test equipment for testing AC-DC circuits, electronics, state-of-the-art computer circuits, computer configuration and related peripheral equipment, servo systems, and microwave systems.

QUALIFICATIONS: Two years of electronics education and/or equivalent plus at least four years' experience in above.

"I might run up against that blank wall [unemployment], but there's no way you're going to find me ten years from now sitting in a slum on 4th Street drawing welfare. I can adapt."

General Supervisor
(Former Divisional Supervisor)
Bettendorf, Iowa

227

Index of Company Names

Advanced Micro Devices, Inc. (AMD)
California: 91
Texas: 201; 212

American Bell
Colorado: Engineering, Design, and
Development Division (ED&D),
127

Apple Computer, Inc.
California: 94
Texas: 189

Ball Aerospace Systems Division
Colorado: 129

Burroughs Wellcome Co.
North Carolina: 176

Coors Porcelain
Colorado: 133

Data General Corporation
California: 100
Massachusetts: 163; 164
North Carolina: 178; 180
Texas: 203

Datapoint Corporation
Texas: 214

Garrett AiResearch Manufacturing Co.
Arizona: Electronic Systems Division,
80

General Electric
North Carolina: Semiconductor
Business Division, 181

W.L. Gore & Associates, Inc.
Texas: Electronics Products Division,
205

Hamilton Test Systems
Arizona: 85

Hewlett-Packard
California: 102, 123
Colorado: 135
Massachusetts: 166

Honeywell, Inc.
Arizona: Large Computer Products
Division, 75
Colorado: Test Instruments Division
(TID), 138; 141
Florida: Avionics Division, 157

Intel Corporation
California: 109

International Business Machines
Corporation (IBM)
Arizona: General Products Division,
82
Colorado: 143
Florida: Information Network
Development and Operation Center,
161
North Carolina: Communication
Products Division, 184
Texas: Federal Systems Division, 192;
Communication Products Division,
207

Kitt Peak National Observatory
Arizona: 87

Litton, Applied Technology
California: 113

Martin Marietta Denver Aerospace
Colorado: 145

Mostek Corporation
Texas: 194

NBI, Inc.
Colorado: 148

Research Triangle Institute
North Carolina: 186

ROLM Corporation
California: 116; MIL-SPEC Computer
Division, 119
Colorado: 150
Texas: Office Systems Division, 209

Sandia National Laboratories
New Mexico: 169